The ASSIST Program

Affective/Social Skills: Instructional Strategies and Techniques

Creating A Caring Classroom

A Validated Washington State Innovative Education Program

Pat Huggins

Sopris West™
EDUCATIONAL SERVICES

A Cambium Learning Company

4093 Specialty Place • Longmont, Colorado 80504 • (303) 651-2829
www.sopriswest.com

28409/10-06

Acknowledgments

I would like to express my appreciation to the following people for their part in the conception and development of the ASSIST Program: to Kateri Brow, Superintendent of Issaquah School District, for her encouragement and support; to Judy Williams, for her constancy, patience, creativity, and unique contributions to the curriculum; to Barbara Ann Baker for her masterful word processing skills and attention to detail in preparing the manuscript; to Hergie (Ernie Hergenroeder) for his permission to use his illustrations. A large share of thanks goes to the following teachers who piloted the ASSIST Program and, through their feedback, helped to make the curriculum more effective:

Issaquah School District
Ruth Adamitz
Terry Adams
Delores Steward
Mary Stolze
Jim Jorden
Cathy Kirkman

North Kitsap School District
Renee Fossom
Becky Sibbet
Pat Jones
Carolyn Russell
Shirley Parrot
Karen Campbell

Shoreline School District
Paula Jones

Bellevue School District
Meryl Thomson

A special thanks to Neale Huggins for his support and advice and editing assistance.

Larry Moen has been instrumental in the revision of this manual, including his contributions in writing, editing, and graphic design.

The ASSIST Program includes many activities and ideas contributed by teachers over the course of several years. We would appreciate any information that would assist in correction of any errors or omissions in acknowledgment of ownership of materials.

Table of Contents

Overview of the ASSIST Program

Affective/Social Skills: Instructional Strategies and Techniques

The ASSIST Program is designed to increase students' growth in self-esteem, selfmanagement, interpersonal relationships, conflict resolution, and emotional understanding. ASSIST manuals provide a complete guide for elementary school teachers and counselors to actively involve students in developing critical personal/social skills. The ASSIST Program can be used as a K-6 developmental school guidance curriculum by following the scope and sequence presented in Appendix B. It can be integrated into regular academic programs, or each manual can stand alone as a curriculum for personal growth or social competence.

The ASSIST curriculum is the result of an extensive review of child development theory and research, a review of existing social/emotional education programs, and the feedback of many teachers and students who participated in the program. ASSIST incorporates concepts and procedures from social learning theory, child psychology, and proven educational practices.

Each field-tested lesson includes:

- A "To the Teacher" section which provides a theoretical background for the lesson concepts;

- A "scripted" lesson that provides the dialogue, examples, and practice necessary to teach the lesson concepts and skills;

- A series of transparency masters which make the lesson concepts accessible to picturesmart students;

- A series of reproducible worksheets which provide opportunities for students to process the lessons; and

- A variety of "Supplementary Activities" designed to encourage the transfer of training.

ASSIST was developed with Title IV-C Innovative Education Funds and was evaluated in elementary school classrooms in four school districts. **Statistically significant gains in self-concept and social skills occurred in eight out of nine assessments.** As a result, ASSIST was validated in Washington State and designated cost-effective and exportable. It is now in the state's "Bank of Proven Practices," a clearinghouse for quality programs.

The ASSIST manuals currently in print include the following:

- ***Building Self-Esteem in the Classroom***—In both the *Primary Version* and the *Intermediate Version* students refine their self-descriptions and acquire an appreciation for their uniqueness. They learn that they are multifaceted and that there are at least seven different ways they can be smart. They learn the cognitive skill of self-encouragement, which enables them to respond to mistakes, failures, or put-downs in a manner which maintains their self-esteem. They learn to take responsibility for their school success by using self-statements to motivate and coach themselves through academic tasks. A unit written for advanced or middle school students is also included in the *Intermediate Version*. (*Primary Version*, 926 pages; *Intermediate Version*, 670 pages)

- ***Creating A Caring Classroom***—This manual includes a collection of strategies designed to promote mutual support and strengthen connections in the classroom. Included are (1) getting-acquainted activities; (2) classroom management procedures; (3) a personal/social behavior scale and behavior improvement strategies for students with special needs; (4) a relaxation training program; and (5) a large collection of activities for establishing a nurturing classroom community. (400 pages)

- ***Helping Kids Find Their Strengths***—This manual is designed to enable students to identify and utilize their strengths. It is based on the combined expertise of the theorists, researchers, and practitioners who worked on the Dependable Strengths Project Team at the University of Washington. Students are able to build their self-esteem not just by positive thinking but by analyzing experiences they're proud of for clues regarding their core strengths. Students share their good experiences, then utilize teacher and peer input to "tease out" the strengths that helped them create those experiences. They learn a large strength vocabulary and are able to prove to themselves and others that they have strengths they can depend on. They use their expanded self-identity as a springboard for new successes. In helping one another find their strengths, students develop a respect for diversity. (713 pages)

- ***Helping Kids Handle Anger***—This manual includes lessons designed to enable students to acknowledge, accept, and constructively express anger. Students learn: (1) to use inner speech to inhibit aggressive behaviors; (2) to use thinking skills for choosing constructive behaviors when angry; (3) appropriate language for expressing anger; (4) a variety of techniques for releasing energy after anger arousal; (5) ways to defuse the anger of others; and (6) a model for resolving classroom conflicts. Role-plays and puppets are utilized to encourage active student involvement. (516 pages)

- ***Helping Kids Handle Put-Downs***—This manual teaches students a repertoire of assertive responses to teasing that will not reinforce their antagonizers. Students learn the art of ignoring; how to surprise aggressors by "agreeing" with them; how to disarm aggressors with humor; and how to deflect aggression with "crazy compliments." These strategies win respect and de-escalate conflict. Students also learn to use self-encouragement to dispel the hurt of put-downs and maintain their self-respect. This volume contains both a *Primary Version* and *Intermediate Version*. (283 pages)

- ***Multiple Intelligences: Helping Kids Discover the Many Ways They're Smart***—The purpose of this manual is to help students understand that they are intellectually multifaceted. They are introduced to a process to assess their own strong intelligences. Students learn that each intelligence is as valuable as any other and gain respect for their own particular strengths, as well as those of others. The lessons in this manual are an expanded version of a unit on multiple intelligence in *Building Self-Esteem in the Classroom*. Additionally, this new manual contains a section of activities linking multiple intelligences with career choices. (333 pages)

- ***Teaching Cooperation Skills***—This manual includes a series of lessons and experiential activities designed to teach students the skills necessary for cooperative learning to take place. Lessons focus on the skills of self-management, listening, collaborative problem solving, and leadership. Students learn to resolve conflicts through negotiation and compromise. Included are 52 activities designed to provide practice of cooperation skills and 55 cooperative academic activities in the major subject areas. (437 pages)

- ***Teaching Friendship Skills***—Both the *Primary Version* and the *Intermediate Version* contain all new lessons and supplementary activities for each grade level. Students identify the behaviors in others which attract them and behaviors which alienate them. They examine their own behavior and determine changes they need to make in order to gain friends. They learn how to curb physical and verbal aggression. They discover that the secret to making friends is to make others feel special, and they practice specific ways to do so. They learn the value of sharing and how to give sincere compliments and apologies. In addition, the *Intermediate Version* focuses on listening, understanding others' perspectives and feelings, and being honest but kind. It also contains 56 activities designed for a "Friendship Center." Each version provides a comprehensive bibliography of children's books on friendship. Puppets, games, role-plays, kinesthetic activities, and goal-setting are used to increase motivation and the transfer of training. (*Primary Version*, 537 pages; *Intermediate Version*, 605 pages)

- ***Helping Kids Handle Conflict***—Through the lessons and activities presented in this manual, students learn to reduce verbal and physical violence through self-control, critical thinking, negotiation, and other strategies. These skills, applied through the Stop, Think, and Pick a Plan (STP) process, help students understand how to handle their own conflicts and when it is appropriate to seek adult assistance. Lessons 1 through 7 teach the STP process, from self-calming techniques, to deciding if it's best to walk away from a situation, to options available once the choice is made to either leave the disagreement or stay and try to work things out. Lesson 8 teaches students how to apply that process when dealing with bullies. (*Primary Version*, 460 pages)

Introduction

One of the most important elements in any classroom is the classroom climate. Research has consistently shown that both teaching and learning improve as a result of a warm and supportive atmosphere in the classroom. If students have positive feelings about being in a certain classroom with other students and with their teacher, they tend to be more motivated toward academic tasks, participate with a higher degree of involvement, and are more likely to derive permanent gain for their efforts. A positive classroom climate can do much to provide an exciting and rich learning experience for everyone involved.

In contrast, the behavior of students in classrooms with a negative climate often undermines educational goals. Students become passive and uncooperative. Their behavior, in many ways, resembles that of people in military or work groups characterized by low morale.

Many people think that the teacher is solely responsible for the quality of the climate in the classroom. They believe if a teacher is kind, warm, sensitive, and honest, a positive climate will automatically develop. To a certain extent, this is true. Yet increasingly there are other classrooms where the behavior and attitudes of some students need to change if a constructive environment is to develop. In these cases more than just the personal characteristics of even the best teacher are needed to improve the functioning of the classroom group. It is necessary to teach students new skills and attitudes.

The purpose of the ideas and activities in this component of the ASSIST Program is to provide a variety of practical procedures that a teacher can use to change a random collection of individual students into a cooperative and productive classroom group. The activities are most appropriate for children from 7-11 years of age, but they have also been used successfully, with some modification, with children both younger and older.

The overall goal of this manual is to help teachers establish a classroom atmosphere characterized by the following:

1. Mutual respect and trust between teacher and students.

2. A mutual alignment of purposes between teacher and students.

3. A feeling on the part of students that they belong to the group.

4. A climate where it is safe for students to express their feelings, inner needs, and hopes.

5. A climate marked by identification, recognition, acceptance, and appreciation of individual and cultural differences.

6. A climate where students readily establish helpful interpersonal relationships and are caring and supportive of one another.

7. A climate where students feel they are able to exercise some measure of influence over their lives in the classroom.

8. A climate in which students have a high degree of involvement in meaningful work.

It can be a tall order to create an environment that frees students to grow socially, emotionally, and academically. Hopefully, the procedures described in this manual will be useful in helping students to develop as "total persons." Many of these ideas and activities are somewhat intuitively known and practiced by teachers. This manual categorizes a wide variety of such strategies, providing teachers with a complete range of procedures to fit their teaching style and belief system, in their efforts to establish a positive classroom climate.

This collection of ideas and activities is divided into five sections. Each of the five sections addresses different avenues for establishing a sense of group togetherness and community in the classroom.

Section A—*Warm-Up Activities* includes 42 activities designed to help students get to know one another and nurture the growth of new friendships. The activities can also be used throughout the school year as "cushion" or "sponge" activities, or as "quick energizers" when a change of pace is needed in the classroom.

Section B—*Climate-Building Activities* includes 29 activities that are designed to help each student feel valued and important to the group. Some are procedures that can be followed on a daily basis, others are for weekly or monthly use, and still others for when an appropriate occasion arises.

Section C—*Individual Behavior Improvement Plan* includes a series of procedures designed to help students eliminate undesirable classroom behavior and strengthen their appropriate behavior. A profile of a student's affective behavior is obtained by rating the student on the *ASSIST Individual/Social Behavior Inventory*. Information and materials are provided to develop for the student specific behavioral objectives (or an IEP for special education students), a plan of reinforcement, a teacher-student contract, and a procedure for measuring progress.

Section D—*Relaxation Techniques* includes detailed ways to help students understand how learning to achieve a relaxation state can lead to improved performance in academic work, sports, and other areas that are important to them. It also provides the teacher with an effective tool for establishing a climate of peace and calm in the classroom. Detailed training scripts are included, as well as a variety of methods for acquiring skills in relaxation.

Section E—*Magic Tricks* includes 15 foolproof tricks that can be taught to the shy, isolated, or less popular students in the classroom. This provides a means whereby their status in the group and self-esteem can be raised by giving them something special to offer the rest of the class. Learning how to do the tricks can also be used as a reinforcement for appropriate classroom behavior. The tricks are particularly useful as a way to get students' attention at the beginning of a lesson. To keep students' attention during a lesson, tell them only those who remain on-task during the lesson will learn how to do the trick at the end of the lesson.

It will be the specific strengths and needs of you and your students that determine the sections of this manual that you use. You may use this manual mainly as a resource. When you have glanced through all the sections, you might then decide which strategies would most productively be implemented first in your class, and begin with those. You may then earmark other sections for use at a later time.

Another approach, and one of the best ways to establish a positive classroom climate, is to directly teach the lessons and involve students in the activities in the various ASSIST manuals. You will substantially impact your classroom climate if you teach students to:

- Accept themselves, focus on their strengths, and meet their goals (see *Building Self-Esteem in the Classroom*).

- Work cooperatively with one another (see *Teaching Cooperation Skills*).

- Maintain healthy friendships (see *Teaching Friendship Skills*).

- Deal appropriately with strong feelings (see *Helping Kids Handle Anger*).

As a result of implementing some of the suggestions and activities in this manual, you should observe not only an improvement in the climate of your classroom, but a corresponding improvement in the attention students bring to learning tasks and in their individual/social skills, plus more personal enjoyment in your teaching.

Section A
Warm-Up Activities

Would you like to be my partner?

List of Warm-Up Activities

**Found on
Page(s)**

Recommendations for first and second graders:

Recommendations for third and fourth graders:

**Found on
Page(s)**

Recommendations for fifth and sixth graders:

Introduction

Research has consistently indicated that teaching and learning improve as a result of "group cohesiveness" in which care and concern for others is a common way of behaving.

If caring relationships are to develop within the classroom, each person will need to be viewed as a unique individual with special opinions, feelings, likes, and dislikes. For a person to be viewed as a distinct individual, he/she will need to tell others about himself/herself. Warm-ups are activities that help students feel more free to share information about themselves and feel "at home" in the classroom. Using warm-ups at the beginning of the school year is a good way to start building a cohesive classroom group. Students often have only a small amount of information about many of their classmates. This can be true even though students may have been in the same classroom in previous years. Through warm-up activities students can begin to appreciate one another in new ways and establish new friendships. Warm-ups help to establish a climate of trust and build a foundation for working together.

Warm-ups can also be used throughout the school year as a filler activity, an "energizer," or whenever a fun change of pace is needed. They are as effective at midyear as at the beginning of school for building group cohesiveness and facilitating friendships.

Games With Names

(Primary/Intermediate Levels)

Objective   Students will learn each others' names and learn about each other through name groups.

Strategy   Group game

Materials   None

Procedure   You have a variety of choices available here. Select one or several that you feel best suit your class.

1. Bill—Bear

    Students sit in a circle. Each student in turn says their first name and then something they like that starts with the same letter as their name. For example, "I'm Bill and I like bears," or "I'm Sue and I like singing." After four or five students have spoken, "quiz" selected students by pointing to the first students and asking what their name is. (If a student has trouble remembering, the student pointed to may say their "like" as a clue to help the student having trouble.) Continue on, four or five students at a time, until you have done the entire group.

    ## Variations

    You may choose instead to have each student say his or her name (and like) and then repeat back all of the previous names that have been given out. Again, use the "likes" as clues.

    You may choose to have instead of the broad category of "likes" a word that begins with the same letter as the name and fits a theme such as foods, animals, or places. For example, "I'm Paul and I like pizza."

2. The Name Chain

    A name chain is one of the most effective methods for helping students to learn each others' names. These steps will help make this activity run smoothly.

First, ask your students to sit in a circle so that each can comfortably see all the students in the group.

Clearly explain the reasons for being involved in this activity. Explain to the students that each person will be asked to say his/her first name and tell the group one thing about himself/herself. They may choose to tell the group something they like to do, something interesting that happened to them recently, and so on. Inform the class that they will be asked to repeat each student's name and the statement made. They will begin with the person who spoke first and stop when they have given their name and have said something about themselves. The first student may say, "I'm Bob, and I went to the beach last weekend." The next student will say, "You're Bob, and you went to the beach last weekend. I'm Sandy, and I like soccer." Because it is a difficult task to learn a large number of names and because having an adult remember their names seems particularly important to children, it is best to have you be the last person to list each student's name and what they have shared with the class.

Next, have everyone take a paper and pencil and change seats. Ask the students to start with a designated individual and go clockwise around the circle, writing down each person's name. It is not necessary to have them list what each student shared. Then, ask for a volunteer who will begin with the person designated as the starting point and slowly give the name of each person in the circle. This recital serves as an opportunity for students to check the accuracy of their list and to learn the names of any students they might have missed.

3. Learning About Names

This activity is excellent as a first get-acquainted activity. Place students in groups of five or six. Briefly lead a discussion on names. You might include comments about how names may reflect cultural heritage, refer to a loved relative, or be chosen because a parent liked the name. The discussion can also focus on how names may evoke positive or negative feelings, depending on how each of us likes our name or what people do with our name. Then, tell students that this activity involves sharing some things about the students' names as a way of becoming better acquainted. Ask students to tell these facts about their names:

- State their full name.

- Do they know how they got their name? For example, were they named for someone? Does the name represent a family heritage or nationality?

- Do they have any nicknames? Who calls them by this name? Do they like the nicknames?

- Do people change their name in any way? For example, is it often shortened, and so on? How do they feel about this?

- Do they like their name? If not, what would they prefer?

- What name do they want used in the class?

After all groups have finished, one student in each group can volunteer to introduce each member of the small group to the entire class, giving the name each student wants to be called in the class.

4.   <u>Names and Desserts</u>

Ask the members of the class to think of their favorite desserts. Then ask for a volunteer to begin by telling his or her name and favorite dessert. Then the members of the class (including yourself) take turns telling their favorite desserts until all have had an opportunity. At the end students can volunteer to try and see how many student names (and even favorite desserts) they can remember.

Variations

Favorite singing group, television show, time of day, thing to do on Saturday morning.

5.   <u>Name Catch</u>

morning meeting
8 - 8:15

A paper ball, or something else soft, is thrown from one member of the circle to another. The student who catches the ball must name the person who threw it to him or her.

If you wish, a discussion may follow as to how students remembered the names of the other students.

6. <u>Zip Zap</u>

The teacher divides the class in half. Each group forms into a circle. One person from each group is selected to be a "Counter."

Counter points at someone in the circle and calls either "zip" or "zap." If he or she calls "zip," the student who is pointed to names the person on the student's right. If the Counter calls "zap," the student who is pointed to names the person on his or her left.

The Counter slowly counts to 10. If the correct name is given within that time, then the game continues and the Counter points to another person.

If the student fails to respond correctly within the count of 10, however, then he or she becomes the new Counter.

At that time, everyone in the circle moves to a new place so the same people are no longer standing next to one another. Play then resumes with the new Counter.

7. <u>Name Chant</u>

This game works like a sports cheer. Have your students sit in a circle with you or a student leader standing in the middle. As the leader randomly points to different sitting students, the group chants in rhythm that student's name. The leader should keep the chanting rhythm going by timely pointing and keep pointing both to new and formerly identified students. This game can be allowed to become loud and can use hand-clapping or foot-pounding as well. The trick is to get a good rhythm going and let this become fun.

8. <u>Pardon Me, You're Wearing My Name</u>

This game is great for students to learn each others' faces.

Write everyone's name down on small pressure-sensitive stickers. Mix these up and distribute them so no one has his or her own name. Ask students to stick the stickers gently onto their faces.

Now everyone is to go around the room trying to find their own name. When a student finds his or her name, that sticker is removed from the other's face and placed onto the student's shirt or dress like a normal name tag. The student who has found his or her name then stays with the person who was wearing that sticker and helps to find that student's name.

9. Your Name Is a Puzzle to Me

This is a good way for primary students to learn each others' names.

Make up name tags for all the students. Cut these tags into four or five pieces and place each set of pieces into an envelope. Now distribute the envelopes, one to each student. Each student then puts his or her puzzle together.

After the students are all done, have them put the puzzle pieces back into the envelopes and hand them to the next person on their left. Repeat putting puzzles together and passing them on until everyone has done several names.

10. Our Class—Word Search

Create a Word Search puzzle grid using the names of all the students in your class. Make copies of this as a handout and have all the students solve the puzzle.

Hint: In making Word Search puzzles, it is easiest if you create them by putting down the longest names first.

11. Back to Back

Make up cards or slips of paper which each have the name of one member of your class and in no particular order, a blue, green, or red sticker dot. Randomly selecting these name tags, tape or pin one onto the back of each student.

Students now must go about the room, copying down both the names and the dot color onto a list. While doing this, each student tries to keep other students from reading the name pinned to his or her own back.

After a set time limit, stop the action. The student with the most complete list (names and correct dot colors) wins. This game is good for providing a lot of physical movement and energy release.

Badges

(Primary Level)

Objective   Students will become acquainted with one another.

Strategy   Group activity

Materials   Star pattern, colored markers

Procedure   Make copies of the star badge on the following page and give each student one. Have students write out some specific things about themselves on the badge and then pin it on themselves. Students can wear their badges throughout the day and read each other's. After students have had a chance to read one another's badges, have a class discussion. Ask each student to tell at least one new thing they learned about a classmate.

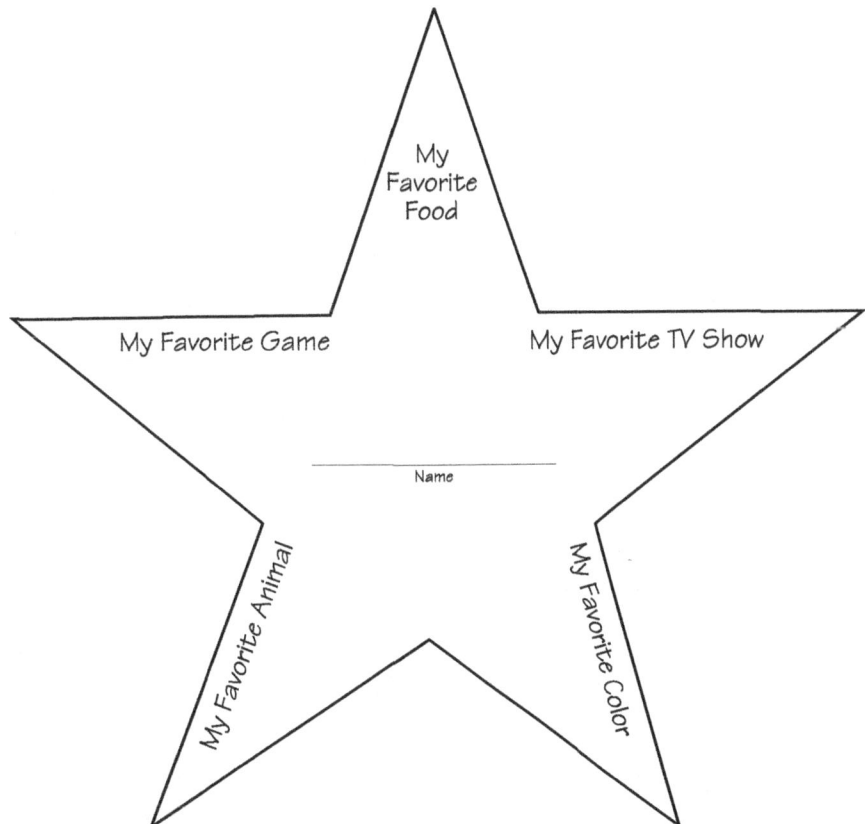

My
Favorite
Food

My Favorite Game   My Favorite TV Show

Name

My Favorite Animal   My Favorite Color

My
Favorite
Food

My Favorite Game

My Favorite TV Show

Name

My Favorite Animal

My Favorite Color

Badges

(Intermediate Level)

Objective   Students will become acquainted with one another.

Strategy   Group activity

Materials   Star Pattern, colored markers

Procedure   Make copies of the intermediate level star badge on the following page and give each student one. As for primary, have students write out some specific things about themselves on the badge and then pin it on themselves. Students can wear their badges throughout the day and read each other's. After students have had a chance to read one another's badges, have a class discussion. Ask each student to tell at least one new thing they learned about a classmate.

A 3" x 5" card will work fine if stars would not be appropriate for your students.

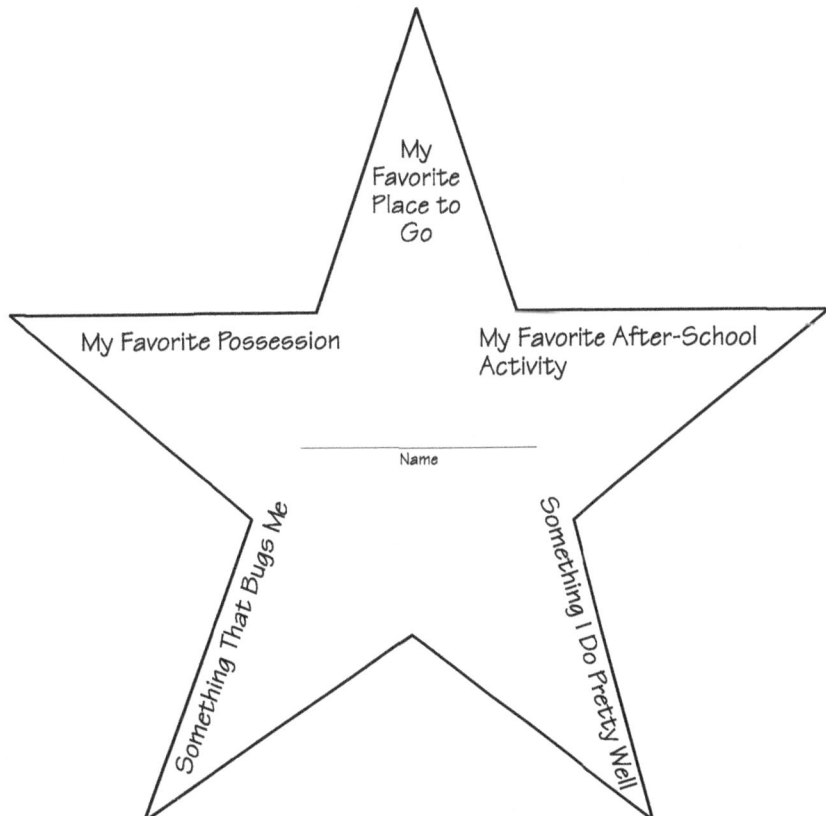

My Favorite Place to Go

My Favorite Possession

My Favorite After-School Activity

Name

Something That Bugs Me

Something I Do Pretty Well

My
Favorite
Place to
Go

My Favorite Possession

My Favorite After-School
Activity

_____
Name

Something That Bugs Me

Something I Do Pretty Well

More Than Name Tags

(Primary/Intermediate Levels)

Objective
Students will learn more about each others' preferences and dislikes.

Strategy
Name tags

Materials
The "More Than Name Tags" handouts (following), pencils

Procedure
Give each student a Name Card copied from the handout following this activity. Ask the students to fill in their name tag as follows:

1. The student's first name is written in the center of the tag.

2. Around the name (in each corner of the tag) students will write their answers to the questions (see below) that you will write on a blackboard or large sheet of paper. (You could also give the questions to the students as a handout.)

Be sure to go over the questions with the students, modeling by giving your answers. As you do this, you may find it helpful to make up a large sample name tag where everyone can see it.

When students have finished their name tags, separate them into small groups. Have each member of the group take turns telling about the items on his or her name tag.

Variations

- Instead of small groups, have your students pair off. Let them share together for a few minutes, then repeat this with new partners. Do this as long as time permits.

- Have your students read each others' name tags silently as they mingle around the room.

- Instead of name tags, you could have students make up posters using this same format.

- Instead of answering questions, have your students simply decorate a large name tag for themselves.

- Instead of writing out answers to these questions, have your students draw pictures or symbols. Going clockwise from upper-right, these pictures might be of

  - a very significant event that happened to you in the last few years;

  - something you currently find frustrating, or a pet peeve;

  - your least favorite food; and

  - your favorite movie.

  (You may instead choose other items for pictures.)

PLACES

Question 1.

Where do you like to go when you want to be alone?

Question 2.

If you could live any place in the world, where would it be?

PEOPLE

Question 1.

If you could be anyone for a day, who would you be?

Question 2.

What person has influenced your life the most?

THINGS

Question 1.

What is your favorite thing to do?

Question 2.

Of all the things you own, which two things do you like best?

DATES

Question 1.

Describe a future date you're looking forward to.

Question 2.

Describe the time you had your best good laugh.

More Than Name Tags

Intermediate

PLACES

1.

2.

PEOPLE

1.

2.

THINGS

1.

2.

DATES

1.

2.

Primary

Something I don't like

1.

2.

Something I like to do in my spare time

1.

2.

My favorite animal

1.

2.

My favorite color

1.

2.

Who Am I?

(Intermediate Level)

Objective   Students will begin interacting with each other by asking questions and giving answers.

Strategy   Question and answer exchange

Materials   Masking tape, felt-tip pen

Procedure   Before the class arrives, write the names of famous people on strips of masking tape so that there is one for each student. The famous names should be easily recognizable to children, such as TV stars, rock singers, athletes, etc. As the class members arrive, put one of the strips of tape on their backs. Each student is then to guess whose name is on his or her back by asking the other class members questions. Inform the class that all questions must be answered "Yes" or "No" and that they cannot ask the same student two questions in a row. Students can remove their strips of tape when they identify their famous person.

Variation

For younger children you may want to tape pictures of animals on their backs, and they are to guess what animal they are.

Source: Adapted from *Relationship Builders*, by Joy Wilt and Bill Watson.

What's on My Back?

(Primary/Intermediate Levels)

Objective   Students will interact with peers they don't know well.

Strategy   Group game.

Materials   Pictures cut from old magazines, pins, or tape

Procedure   Divide students into two groups by having them number off one, two, etc. Pin or tape a picture on the backs of those students who are "number ones." Have them select a "number two" that they don't know very well for a partner. The partners go behind the individuals who chose them and look at the picture on their backs. Then they give clues about the picture, and the students with the picture try to guess what the picture is. If time, you can pin pictures on the backs of "number twos." Have students choose new partners and reverse the process.

Welcome Game

(Primary Level)

Objectives   Students will get to know the names of their classmates.

Strategy   Game activity

Materials   The "Welcome Game" card handout (following), pencil

Procedure   Review the Welcome Game handout.

The format for this game is similar to bingo. Each student is provided with a "Welcome Game" card. The object of the game is to be the first person to have an entire row filled with classmates' names, creating a "Welcome" (bingo). Each student may write his or her own name in one square and the word "Free" in two squares anywhere on the board; however, only one free space may be used in a "Welcome." Students move around the room in silence, having others sign their names in a square. When a student has names written in each box in a row going either across, up and down, or diagonally, he says "Welcome."

If the student can then identify each person on the "Welcome" line, that student is the winner. If not, the game continues until another person gets a "Welcome." NOTE: The example game board has 36 squares. Adjust your board according to the number of students in your class. You will need one square per student, plus adding some free spaces to make an even grid. Add or subtract rows as needed to achieve this. Some additional game strategies and rules that should be discussed prior to the game are:

1. Don't sign your name on someone else's card in a row that is almost full.

2. The activity must be done without talking. If talking occurs, that student is "frozen" out of the game.

3. Children may want to wait to fill in their own name and free spaces as they get close to a "Welcome." Otherwise, others will avoid signing in that row.

Variation

You can have students walk around and have their classmates sign their cards until the cards are full. Then you read off student names randomly. Just as in Bingo, whenever a student is able to cover an entire row on his card, he calls out "welcome," but then must identify each person as he reads off all the names in his row.

Welcome Game

The rules to this game are similar to bingo. When the game begins, you quietly walk around the room and give your card to classmates to sign their names. When you have **six** names across, up and down, or diagonally, you say, "Welcome." You must then point to each person as you read their name from your "Welcome" line. **You win only if you can identify all people who have signed on that line.** Don't forget to fill in two spaces with the word "Free." Remember, when you're writing your name on someone's paper, try to keep him/her from getting a "Welcome" first by not signing in a row that is nearly filled.

Classmates' Names Bingo

(Primary/Intermediate Levels)

Objective   Students will gain greater awareness of each other's names.

Strategy   Bingo game.

Materials   Bingo card handout (following), pencils

Procedure   Pass out to each student a black Bingo card. Use the handout or adapt it by adding or removing sets of rows and columns. For example, if you have 33 students, use a 6" x 6" grid to get 36 spaces and then blank out three "free" squares.

Ask students to look around the room and fill their classmate's names randomly into the squares. When everyone has a different name in each of the squares, it is time for the Bingo to begin.

From a hat or box, randomly pull out students' names. Players then mark an "X" through their game card square with that name. When a player creates a row of "X"s vertically, horizontally, or diagonally (with or without "free" squares), he or she has a bingo.

You may decide to play until everyone has at least one bingo, or repeat the game with new arrangements of the names.

	B	I	N	G	O
1					
2					
3			FREE		
4					
5					

Is There Someone in This Class Who . . . ?

(Primary/Intermediate Levels)

Objective   Students will become better acquainted with their classmates and realize that each person is someone special.

Strategy   Group activity

Materials   The primary level, "Who in This Class . . .?" handout (following); The intermediate level, "What Person in the Class . . .?" handout (following)

Procedure   Pass out the activity sheets and explain to students that the boxes on the sheet contain special qualities that different people in the class have. Explain to students that they are to walk quietly around the room and secretly find people who have the quality in the box. They will then ask that person to sign his or her name in the square. Remember to get the signature! When you find a person, keep it a secret. Let your classmates find out for themselves.

You may wish to set a time limit to end the activity or you may wish to stop when several students have completed their sheet. Explain that the following guidelines should be observed: No rushing around or running, use only quiet voices, ask questions politely, and use no put-downs.

The following questions can be used for a class discussion after students have done this activity:

1.   What was the hardest square to find?

2.   What was the most surprising thing you found out about a classmate?

3.   Let's find out about the special people in our class. Whose name do you have in Square #1—a person who has more than one dog? (Intermediate Level), or a person who has blue eyes? (Primary Level). Continue asking about the people found for each square.

4. How many of you got names in 10 boxes? Twenty boxes? All the boxes?

5. What statement was the hardest to get a signature for? Can anyone else in the class fill this category?

Is There Someone in This Class Who . . . ?

(Primary Level)

Walk quietly around the room and find a person who fits the description in the box. Have that person write his or her name in the box.

Find a person who . . .

has blue eyes.	has a birthday this month.	is taller than you are.
has a dog and a cat.	is new to your school.	was born in your town.
has a tooth missing.	wears glasses.	can whistle.
has been on a camping trip.	is the only child in the family.	is on a sports team.

Is There Someone in This Class Who . . . ?

(Intermediate Level)

Walk quietly around the room and find a person who fits the description in the box. Have that person write his or her name in the box. When you find this person, keep it a secret and let your classmates find out for themselves. Have only one signature to a box.

Find a person who . . .

owns more than one dog.	visited a relative outside the state last summer.	caught a fish last summer.	was born outside this state.	went to visit a grandparent last summer.
went camping in the past year.	chooses chocolate as favorite flavor.	has the same middle name as someone else in this room.	moved to a different house within the past year.	has ridden on a train or plane.
has more than two brothers.	shares a bedroom.	uses your same brand of toothpaste.	has had a broken bone.	plays a musical instrument.
likes hamburgers better than pizza.	has the most freckles.	lives on the same street as another classmate.	does not have a middle name.	has traveled outside the United States.
has lived in the same house all of his or her life.	can stand on one foot for 10 seconds.	has more than nine letters in his or her last name.	has a dog and a cat.	plays baseball or soccer on a team.

"Who in This Class?" Bingo

(Primary/Intermediate Levels)

Objective   Students will become acquainted with members of the class and with the teacher.

Strategy   Bingo game

Materials   Primary or intermediate BINGO handouts (following), pencil

Procedure   Pass out a primary or intermediate level "People Bingo" card to each student.

Have students then go around to each other trying to find those whose characteristics fit the ones stated in the bingo boxes. When they find a match, they are to write that student's name in the box.

Students are to fill in as many squares as they can.

You may elect to have a prize (or recognition) for the student who gets the first bingo and/or the most squares filled in on his or her handout.

(Primary Level)

Find a person who . . .

	B	I	N	G	O
1	has more than 3 brothers and sisters.	has brown eyes.	owns an all white cat.	has the same color eyes as you.	has seen the same movie at least 3 times.
2	likes to fix things.	rides a bike to school.	loves comic books.	lives in an apartment.	has two sisters.
3	has blonde hair.	collects rocks.	is wearing blue socks.	has a middle name of Ann.	can cross their eyes.
4	likes the comics.	loves airplanes.	likes to draw.	is left-handed.	loves to laugh.
5	wears glasses.	has a pet.	is an only child.	enjoys liver for a meal.	likes to eat fish.

(Intermediate Level)

Find a person who . . .

B	I	N	G	O
1 likes broccoli.	likes to read mystery stories.	has a pet gerbil.	is a sports addict.	has an insect or stamp collection.
2 has won an award.	has been outside the United States.	likes winter better than summer.	likes milk with popcorn.	has 2 or more cats.
3 likes hamburgers better than pizza.	is good at art.	FREE	plays the piano.	walks to school.
4 likes to sew.	is wearing jeans.	is taller than you.	has never missed a day of school.	knows their times tables to 12.
5 likes the same radio station you do.	delivers newspapers.	plays chess.	can speak two languages.	is on a team.

Worsts and Favorites: Get-Acquainted Questions

(Primary/Intermediate Levels)

Objective   Students will learn more about each other through engaging in cooperative actions.

Strategy   Team/group activity

Materials   The "Get Acquainted Questions #1 and #2" handout (following), pencils

Procedure   Choose from the following handouts the one you feel is most appropriate for your class. Give each student a copy and allow them a few minutes to fill it in.

Next, divide the class into groups. In each group students begin by each telling the group what his or her answer to the first question was. Students will then talk about their answers with each other. They will then repeat this procedure for all the remaining questions.

Have each group select one of its members. This person's answers are then read to the rest of the class, who tries to guess who the student is who wrote those answers. Do this once for each group.

You may want to ask the large group these questions.

1. Which two of your favorite things would you be most willing to give up?
   Which would be the most difficult to give up?

2. Which five favorites will most likely change five years from now?

3. Which of your favorites is the oldest?
   Which favorite is the most recent?

4. Which of your favorite things do you think would be the most different from other classmates?

5. Which favorite would most likely continue the rest of your life?

Get-Acquainted Questions: Favorites

What is your favorite TV program? _____

What is your favorite thing to eat? _____

What are your favorite games to play? _____

_____

If you could go anywhere in the world, where would you go? _____

_____

What are your favorite books? _____

_____

What is your favorite subject in school? _____

Do you have a pet? If so, what is it? If you don't have a pet, what kind of pet would be your favorite? _____

What is your favorite movie? _____

What is your favorite song? _____

Do you have any favorite hobbies? _____

_____

Get-Acquainted Questions: Worsts

The worst thing that has ever happened to me was _____

_____.

The worst food in the world is _____.

The worst show on TV is _____.

The worst movie I have ever seen is _____.

The worst thing about school is _____.

The worst song I have ever heard was _____.

The worst thing that I have ever done is _____.

The worst thing I can think of is _____.

The worst place I've ever been _____.

The worst trip I ever took was _____.

The worst toy I ever had was _____.

The worst thing about being my age is _____.

The worst thing about being a girl is _____.

The worst thing about being a boy is _____.

Cooperative Trivia Search

(Primary/Intermediate Levels)

Objective Students will learn more about others and find interesting similarities.

Strategy Trivia search

Materials The "Trivia Search!" handout (following); 3" x 5" cards, pencils

Procedure This activity is done in two parts, with preparation time before each part.

Select enough 3" x 5" cards so that each member of the class will have one. On each card mark at random 4 numbers from 1 to 20.

Pass out to all students one of these 3" x 5" cards and a copy of the "Trivia Search!" worksheet. Tell students to write answers on the card to only those questions from the worksheets whose numbers are written on the cards. Each student will then have four answers on his or her card. Next, students are to write their full name on the cards and hand them back to you.

Take these answers and make a new worksheet, creating questions from the students' answers. Thus you might have questions such as "Whose favorite possession is their grandfather's old jackknife?" or "Who was born in Selma, Alabama?" Select questions that will lead to a specific class member. You may need to combine questions to do this. For example, "Whose favorite animal is a bear and favorite sport is skiing?"

When you have completed your grid of questions, make copies of this new worksheet and distribute to the class. Divide the class into pairs or teams. Each team will cooperate to find the answers to each question. This may be done in class, or you may designate other times for it to be accomplished.

- Set a deadline.

- When the deadline is reached, ask to see how well the teams did.

- What was the hardest clue to solve?

- Who had the most correct answers?

- What did they learn about their classmates that was fun or surprising?

Trivia Search!

1. What is your favorite possession?

2. What is your favorite TV show?

3. What is your favorite book?

4. What is your favorite animal?

5. What is your favorite radio station?

6. What is your favorite sport?

7. Who is your favorite female singer?

8. Who is your favorite sports star?

9. What is your middle name?

10. Where were you born?

11. What is your favorite unusual name for a pet?

12. What is your favorite month?

13. What is the name of the street you live on?

14. What is your favorite movie?

15. How many brothers do you have? Sisters?

16. What is your favorite of the gifts you ever received?

17. What is your favorite candy?

18. What do you hate to have to do on a Saturday?

19. What do you think is the worst toy?

20. What do you think is the worst sports team?

Get-Acquainted Cards

(Primary Level)

Objective   Students will get to know more about each other.

Strategy   Group Warm-up

Materials   The "Get Acquainted" cards handout (following)

Procedure   Cut up most or all the cards on the following pages and put them into a
container. One at a time, have students draw a card and respond to it.
Students may draw a second card if they do not like their first choice.
Cards are not returned to the box. Continue until all students have
responded at least once.

Cut cards as before. Create a "Student-of-the-Week" bulletin board or
other such area. Each week select a student for this honor. He or she
will select 10–15 of the cards to complete. These are put up on the
board or glued to construction paper along with other mementos, pictures, artwork, etc., that will help the rest of the class get to know the
student better.

Something I wish I had more time for is . . . .

The hardest thing I've ever done was . . . .

Something that really bugs me . . . .

The person I admire most is . . . .

My two favorite possessions are . . . .

An unfulfilled ambition I have is . . . .

One of my most embarrassing moments was when . . . .

My favorite comic strip is . . . .

My favorite pizza topping is . . . .

If I could be any place on vacation, I'd go to . . . .

The best thing that ever happened to me . . . .

My favorite place . . . .

What I like best about being my age . . . .

T.V. shows I like to watch . . . .

My idea of a perfect Saturday . . . .

My favorite sports are . . . .

My pets are . . . .

Favorite professional football team . . . .

My favorite color is . . .

If I could travel anywhere I'd go . . . .

The thing I would like most to get as a present is . . . .

My favorite food is . . . .

My hobbies are . . . .

If I could be any animal I'd be . . . .

One thing in the world I'd change if I had the power . . . .

My favorite place to eat is . . . .

What I would do if I won a lot of money . . . .

(Add your own)

(Add your own)

(Add your own)

The worst thing about my age . . .

Something that I have worked hard to get . . .

I could not believe my luck when . . . .

The best advice I've ever received . . . .

The kind of people I like for friends are . . . .

My favorite music group . . .

My favorite subject in school . . .

How I would like to be remembered . . .

One of the funniest moments of my life was when . . .

My favorite room in my home is . . .

I was named after . . .

My favorite movie . . .

I don't like it when . . .

The craziest thing I've ever done . . .

A time I felt proud of myself was when . . .

I always feel good when . . .

Two of my favorite things are . . .

I feel happiest when . . .

What really bothers me is . . .

I'll never forget . . .

I like the sound of . . .

It's hard for me to . . .

I hate it when . . .

The most meaningful gift I've ever received is . . .

"Who Are We?" Inventory

(Primary/Intermediate Levels)

Objective   Students will become acquainted with one another.

Strategy   Warm-Up

Materials   The "Who Are We?" list (below)

Procedure   Read the following list (or a modified one) to the class. After each item, students raise their hands if the statement applies to them. They may, of course, pass on any question, but they should be encouraged to raise their hands and see who else in the class does the same. You can set the tone by also responding.

There are many possibilities for expanding this list into discussion and further activities. You may wish to pause along the way and let students add statements of their own. Students also may wish to create their own lists for use throughout the year.

"Who Are We?" List

1.   I like candy with nuts.
2.   I like to stay up late.
3.   I have flown in a plane.
4.   I have been in a bus in a city.
5.   I have been on a farm.
6.   I have a pet.
7.   I like tangerines.
8.   I am the oldest child in my family.
9.   I am the youngest child in my family.
10.   I am a middle child in my family.
11.   My grandmother or grandfather lives near me.
12.   I can climb a tree.
13.   I can roller skate.
14.   I have my own room.
15.   I wish I could fly.
16.   I am afraid of bugs.
17.   I have been to camp.
18.   I have been to a different state.
19.   I have seen the ocean.
20.   I can ride a two-wheeler with no hands.
21.   I like the winter.

22. I like to jump in fallen leaves.
23. I have played in the snow.
24. I have a secret hiding place.
25. I like to go berry picking.
26. I once won a prize or award.
27. I have been on a team.
28. I have not broken a bone.
29. I have had an operation.
30. I have a great-grandparent.
31. I watch cartoons on Saturday mornings.
32. I get an allowance for doing chores.
33. I make my own breakfast.
34. I know how to swim.
35. I have caught a fish.
36. I like pizza.
37. I like spinach.
38. I like McDonald's hamburgers better than my mother's.
39. I like to paint.
40. I make models.
41. I catch bugs.
42. I can shoot a bow and arrow.
43. I love chocolate ice cream.
44. I have been to a symphony concert.
45. I like to dress up.
46. I have a library card.
47. I like rock 'n' roll.
48. I like my middle name.
49. I have been to a professional ball game.

Things We Have in Common

(Primary Level)

Objective   Students will become acquainted with each other by interacting in various groups.

Strategy   Group activity

Materials   None

Procedure   Have students form groups according to common characteristics. As you read the characteristics, have students get up and come to a certain area of the room for a few seconds and observe who is standing with them. As you change the characteristics, ask them to notice if any one person was in all of their groups. Among the possible group characteristics:

1.   All students who have blue eyes, gray/green eyes, or brown eyes.

2.   All students who have freckles (or no freckles).

3.   All students who have a birthday between January and _____.

4.   All students who have stripes on their clothing.

5.   All students who are wearing jeans.

6.   All students whose names start with "J" (or any other letter of the alphabet).

7.   All students who share a bedroom with a brother or sister.

8.   All students who are wearing clothes that have long sleeves.

9.   All students who are wearing red (or any other color).

Source: *Relationship Builders*, by Joy Wilt and Bill Watson.

Keeping the Beat

(Primary Level)

Objective   Students will get to know each other through quickly-formed groups.

Strategy   Group game

Materials   Drum, gong, or similar noisemaker

Procedure   This is a fun, simple, and active way to encourage group identity and learning things about fellow classmates.

Have your students stand in a circle. You or a designated leader has the drum (gong, or other such loud noisemaker). Explain to your students that they are to count how many times the drum is hit. When the drum stops, students are to form groups containing the same number of students as there were drumbeats. When they have the correct number, students join hands and sit down. (If there are an odd number of students left over, assign these to any existing group.)

Once students are in a group, have them answer to each other a get-acquainted question such as "The thing that bugs me the most is . . ." or "My favorite song is . . ." or "I have a pet or stuffed animal whose name is _____."

After students have had a moment to exchange brief answers, ask them to stand again and find a place between two different people than before they sat down. Now beat the drum and repeat the group-creation process. Do this quickly and repeatedly, varying the group sizes and asking a new question each time.

Similarities

(Primary Level)

Objective   Students will learn a great number of things about fellow classmates and will discover shared attributes.

Strategy   Comparison inventory game

Materials   The "Similarities" handout (following), pencil

Procedure   Ask students to find a partner whom they do not know well. Give each student a copy of the handout and allow them enough time to answer the list of questions.

Next, tell the students that they are to compare their answers with each other and circle any similarities. After allowing time for this, then ask the pairs to add up the number of similarities. The pair with the most similarities wins a recognition of your choice.

Rejoin into a larger group. Lead the students in discussing what they found out in this activity about getting to know someone else better and discovering things in common. Did they have any surprises?

Variation

For primary students you may wish to change the handout questions somewhat. One good set of questions primary students like is answering what they think "the worst" things are. The activity in this section called Cooperation Group Warm-ups has questions you could use.

Similarities

1. My favorite article of clothing is _____

2. My favorite radio station is _____

3. My favorite color is _____

4. My favorite ice cream flavor is _____

5. My favorite snack is _____

6. My favorite board game is _____

7. My favorite song is _____

8. My favorite TV show is _____

9. My favorite school subject is _____

10. My favorite sandwich is _____

11. My favorite toothpaste is _____

12. My favorite pizza topping is _____

13. My favorite comic strip is _____

14. My favorite book is _____

15. My favorite store is _____

16. My favorite breakfast food is _____

17. My favorite home-cooked meal is _____

18. My favorite out-of-town place to visit is _____

19. My favorite television star is _____

20. My favorite animal at the zoo is _____

Similarity Pairs

(Intermediate Level)

Objective   The students will be able to recognize and identify shared attributes.

Strategy   Interview/discussion

Materials   Pencil and paper

Procedure   Have the students pair off for 4 or 5 minutes. Have the students list all the things they have in common. Then let the students get in groups of four and repeat the activity. After 5 minutes, come back together as a class and let one person from each group list things that he or she had in common with other members in the group. Afterwards, let the students discuss commonality among the groups.

So then: We all like pepperoni pizza, soccer, kittens, and scary movies!

Lining Up by Similarities

(Primary/Intermediate Levels)

Objective   Students will repeatedly be reminded of similarities among themselves.

Strategy   All lining-up times

Materials   None

Procedure   One way to encourage friendships is to help students see similarities between themselves and others. A powerful way to easily include this awareness in daily activities is to do so whenever students are asked to line up.

Instead of your usual line-up procedures, ask students to line up by different and more personal criteria. For example, one day you might ask students to line up depending on the number of brothers and sisters they have. Another day it might be by eye color, favorite vegetable, or birthdate. Use any criteria you want, but keep varying what you use so as to bring out new similarities. This also works to bring students with similarities into physical proximity, which adds another step toward developing friendships.

Variation

Use birthdates in the following manner.

Tell the class they are to arrange themselves in one line according to their birthdates, with the youngest at one end and the oldest at the opposite end. When they are done, check for accuracy by going down the line, starting with the youngest and asking each person to give his birthdate.

NOTE: If you have children in class who have been "held back," you may wish to do this activity by month and day of birth only, excluding year of birth from consideration.

If I Could Be . . .

(Intermediate Level)

Objective   Students will get to know one another better through imaginative metaphors.

Strategy   Writing activity and discussion

Materials   The "If I Could Be . . ." handout (following), pencils

Procedure   This activity is designed to uncover similarities among students in a fun and safe way for them to be self-divulging.

Give to each student a copy of the handout. Model a few random questions with your own preferences, then allow students time to complete their own answers.

Next, lead a discussion. Ask students how they responded, allowing volunteers to explain their reasons. You may also wish to ask "Who also said they would be a . . .?" and ask some of those students what their reasons were, if different.

Finally, put the preference lists up where other students can see them.

Variation

This preference inventory can be used for a number of other activities and games. It can be the basis of "Guess who?" games. An especially fun game is "Mystery Groups." Use student's answers to place students in groups which all share only one preference. Have these students then use the inventory to find out what one preference they all share in common. When they find their shared preference, ask students to discuss among themselves their reasons. They might also create a group slogan or poster; for example "The Guitar Group—We're first string."

Name _____

If I Could Be . . .

If I could be any animal, I'd be a(n) _____,
because _____.

If I could be a bird, I'd be a(n) _____,
because _____.

If I could be an insect, I'd be a(n) _____,
because _____.

If I could be a flower, I'd be a(n) _____,
because _____.

If I could be a tree, I'd be a(n) _____,
because _____.

If I could be a piece of furniture, I'd be a(n) _____,
because _____.

If I could be a musical instrument, I'd be a(n) _____,
because _____.

If I could be a building, I'd be a(n) _____,
because _____.

If I could be a car, I'd be a(n) _____,
because _____.

If I could be a fish, I'd be _____,
because _____.

If I could be a person from the past, I'd be _____,
because _____.

If I could be a bumper sticker, I'd say _____,
because _____.

If I could be a sports star, I'd be _____,

because _____.

If I could be a rock star, I'd be _____,

because _____

If I could be a TV star, I'd be _____,

because _____.

If I could be a movie star, I'd be _____,

because _____.

If I could be a character in a book, I'd be _____,

because _____.

If I could be any color, I'd be _____,

because _____ .

Ice Cream or Hot Sauce?

(Primary Level)

Objective   Students will get to know each other better and find areas where they share thinking.

Strategy   Sharing choices on paired words

Materials   The "Ice Cream or Hot Sauce" handout (following)

Procedure   This is a good community builder that opens a group up to each other through creating an awareness of similarities in a nonthreatening way.

Copy and pass out the handout to each of the students. Ask them to circle the word of the pair that they feel better describes them. For example, they might say "I am more like a Lamborghini (Italian sports car) than a Jeep" or "I am more like a violin than a trumpet." Emphasize that there are no "right" or "wrong" answers—they should put down their own choices. Emphasize also that they are not picking which of the two is their favorite, but which one they feel is more like them.

After the students have finished circling their choices, lead a group discussion. Ask "Who here circled that they are more like a Jeep?" and then "Who circled they are more like a Lamborghini?" Have both choices raise hands. Encourage students to explain why they selected the word they did.

Continue on through the rest of the list in the same fashion.

Ice Cream or Hot Sauce?

Listed below are two columns of words that describe people. Circle the word from each pair that you feel better describes you.

I am more like . . .

Ice Cream	Hot Sauce	Gazelle	Snail
Day	Night	Violin	Trumpet
Jeep	Lamborghini	Morning	Evening
Rainy Day	Sunny Day	Wax	Rock
Moonlight	Firelight	Comedian	Lawyer
The Mountains	The Desert	Coal	Diamond
Marathon Runner	Sprinter	Lamb	Fox
Silk	Flannel	News Report	Soap Opera
Dove	Eagle	Noise	Quiet
Tug Boat	Sailboat	Indoor	Outdoor
Easy Chair	Wood Bench	Hot Chocolate	Iced Tea
Oil Painting	Snapshot	Rock Music	Country Music
Team Sports	Individual Sports	Radio	TV
River	Lake		
Paved Highway	Rocky Road		
Hand	Eye		
Lock	Key		
Tire	Steering Wheel		
Arrow	The Bow		
Music	The Dancer		
House	Tent		
Fall	Spring		
Warm Beaches	Snowy Mountains		

What's My Line?

(Primary/Intermediate Levels)

Objective   Students will learn more about each other and become more self-disclosive.

Strategy   Group game

Materials   The "What's My Line" handout (following)

Procedure   Students seem to greatly enjoy the random nature in which questions are selected in this activity. They find it more exciting and surprising to have individually different questions.

You may do this activity in either of two ways. You may select the questions yourself from the handout "What's My Line?," or you may give the students copies of the handout and let them make the selections. In either case, the selector chooses his or her question by closing his or her eyes and running a finger up and down the page. When eyes are opened, the question pointed to is the one that will be answered.

Select a new student and new question until all students have had a chance. When answering questions, the question should first be read out loud and then the answer given.

You may choose at the end of the activity to comment on certain answers or on how interesting every person is.

What's My Line?

I like my . . .

I like to pretend I . . .

I would like a great big . . .

It's hard for me to . . .

On Saturdays, I like to . . .

I feel silly when . . .

I'm sure glad I . . .

Sometimes I'm afraid of . . .

A funny thing that happened in our family was . . .

When I grow up, I . . .

I'm pretty good at . . .

I hate it when . . .

At school, I like to . . .

My family likes to . . .

I am afraid to . . .

I laugh when . . .

Two of my favorite things are . . .

I don't like to . . .

Once someone helped me by . . .

I would hate to lose . . .

I love to give . . .

I'd like to say a good thing about . . .

I like to play . . .

When people get angry, they should . . .

Something I once did all by myself was . . .

If I could be invisible, I would . . .

I was really scared once when . . .

I always feel good when . . .

I once got hurt when . . .

I was very happy the time that . . .

My face has a big smile when . . .

I hate to eat . . .

I would not like to live without . . .

I wish I could . . .

I wish people would stop . . .

I like the sound of . . .

If I had a million dollars, I would . . .

I feel sad when . . .

If I could do anything I wanted, I would . . .

I hope that . . .

I would like to learn how to . . .

If I were a giant, I would . . .

I really like . . .

What really bothers me is . . .

I'll never forget . . .

I like the way I . . .

Two things I like about myself are . . .

I sometimes get mad when . . .

I would not like to have . . .

I feel happiest when . . .

If I were a bird, I would . . .

I feel bad when . . .

I would like a magic ring that . . .

School would be better if . . .

I feel important when . . .

I would like to say something nice to . . .

I would be happier if . . .

If I have my own children someday, I'll be sure to . . .

I just love . . .

I need more . . .

If I were older, I would . . .

I would like someone to help me . . .

I love to eat . . .

I don't like it when . . .

I am very good at . . .

At night I like to . . .

I'd use a magic wand to . . .

You can tell when someone likes you by . . .

If I were a teacher, I would . . .

The best time for me is when . . .

If I had very long legs, I would . . .

I'm the kind of person who . . .

I look best when . . .

I just love to . . .

I wish I could change . . .

I don't like it when people . . .

I sometimes wonder if . . .

I would like to give a present of _____ to _____.

One of the best things about me is . . .

When I was little . . .

I like going home because . . .

I feel happy when people . . .

If I were very tiny, I would . . .

I wish someone would give me a gift box containing . . .

I felt like crying when . . .

Something at home I like very much is . . .

I know how to . . .

Someday I would like to help solve the problem of . . .

I am happiest when . . .

My family likes the way I . . .

The best thing about school is . . .

It was hard to do it, but I finally . . .

The best thing about a pet is . . .

After school I . . .

Some people like the way I . . .

Name the Person

(Intermediate Level)

Objective   Students will learn more about each other in a fun way.

Strategy   Team game

Materials   3" x 5" cards, pencils, scoring sheet

Procedure   Write the questions below (or use the alternate questions, following) on a blackboard or large sheet of paper. Next, divide the students into two teams. Give each team member a 3" x 5" card.

Now read off the questions and have the students number and write down their individual answers on their own 3" x 5" cards. Model the activity using your own responses to the questions. The questions are:

1. If I was an animal I'd be a(n) _____.

2. Is my hair color blonde or red, or is it black or brown?

3. Does my last name begin with a letter from A to L or from M to Z?

4. One unusual fact about me is _____.

5. My favorite dessert is _____.

6. If I could teach the class I'd teach about _____.

Collect each team's cards into separate containers. Now, alternating teams, have each student draw a card and read off the answers to the questions. Use the blackboard as a prompt.

As each card is read, the opposite team is to guess who the card identifies. Teams get three guesses for each card. Identifying the person on the first guess scores 5 points, on the second guess 3 points, and on the last 1 point.

Continue on with the play until all students' cards have been read.

Variation (Alternate Questions for 3" x 5" Card Answers)

Mix your questions between easy and hard ones to match the ability level of your group.

Easy Questions

- Am I wearing tennis shoes (jeans, etc.) today?

- Do I usually sit in the first three rows of the class?

- Am I wearing something blue today?

- What kind of pet do I have?

- What is my most favorite food? Least favorite?

Hard Questions

- If I was a musical instrument, I'd be a _____.

- If I was a bird, I'd be a _____.

- If I was an insect, I'd be a _____.

- If I was a plant, I'd be a _____.

- The school work I'm proudest about doing is _____.

- The thing I like most to see on my way home from school is _____.

- If could travel anywhere, I'd go to _____.

- If I could do one thing for another person it would be to _____.

Variation (Small Group Team Building)

Let students score points based on the individual characteristics of each member of their own small group. Some sample scoring questions might be:

- What month is your birthday?

  Score 1 point for Sept.-Dec.
  Score 2 points for Jan.-Mar.
  Score 3 points for Apr.-Jun.
  Score 4 points for Jul.-Aug.

- Score 1 point for each different state where group members were born.

- Add your total number of pets for the group. Score 1 point for each.

- Score 1 point for each brother or sister group members have.

- Score 1 point for each operation a group member has had.

- Score 2 points for each group member who is new to this school this year.

- What color are your socks?

  Score 1 point for no socks.
  Score 2 points for white or blue socks.
  Score 3 points for gray, black, or red.
  Score 4 points for all other colors.

You may choose to make up new questions that suit your specific class. Compare point totals between groups.

Something About Me Nobody Knows

(Primary/Intermediate Levels)

Objective   Students will become better acquainted with one another.

Strategy   Question and answer exchange

Materials   Two copies of grid handout (following)

Procedure   Ask the students to think of something about themselves that the other members of the class are not aware of. Examples are: "I have 30 cousins," "My mother is a nurse," "I hate shots," "I was born in Germany," "I broke both front teeth when I was eight," "I'm allergic to milk," "I collect _____," etc.

Have students write this fact on a piece of paper, but tell them not to divulge any secrets they don't want others to know. They should sign their names.

Take the grids (you may want to run them off back-to-back) and write one "secret" in each box. Then make as many copies of the grids as you have students and give each student a copy. Ask them to go around the classroom and try to find out who wrote each statement. Tell them to write that person's name under the statement in the box. The student who first fills in all the names wins the game!

NOTE: If some students are absent, look up what their "secret" was. Then cross out that box, so the students playing the game know not to look for that person.

I like to do jumps on roller skates.

Something About Me Nobody Knows

Guess Which Is True

(Primary/Intermediate Levels)

Objective   Students will learn more about each other through an activity emphasizing uniqueness.

Strategy   Guessing game

Materials   Individual pieces of paper, pencils

Procedure   This game and its variations can bring to light fascinating facts about students that might otherwise go completely undiscovered. Pass out the papers to students or have them use their own paper.

Explain to your students that the purpose of this game is to guess which unusual statements about their classmates are true. Each student is to write down on his sheet of paper one true statement about him or herself and two statements that are false. These can be written down in any order. The true statement should be about something that the other students would not be likely to know. For example: "I once met the governor of this state" or "I have a collection of fossil shells." After everyone has written their statements, they will each in turn read these to the rest of the class. The group guesses each time which one is the true statement.

You may choose to make this into a contest by having students receive one point for every classmate who makes an incorrect guess. The student with the most points wins.

Variations

- STORIES

    In this variation students will each tell one story about themselves that may or may not be true. Listeners guess if it is fact or fiction.

- RIDDLES

Students write a riddle about themselves on a piece of paper. These riddles are put into a box. Each student then draws out one of the riddles and reads it to the class. Everyone then tries to guess who the riddle is about.

These riddles should have at least four unique facts about the student. An example would be:

- I was born in Michigan.

- I have brown hair.

- I have a pet cat named "Snowy."

- I don't like math or singing.

- Who am I?

Another good riddle activity is to have each student write on a piece of paper a list of 10 words (adjectives) that they believe are descriptive of themselves. Other students try to guess their identity using this list.

Get-Acquainted Grab Bag

(Intermediate Level)

Objective   Students will talk about themselves so that others can get to know them better.

Strategy   Extemporaneous speaking

Materials   Grocery bag, miscellaneous small objects

Procedure   Before beginning the activity, collect an assortment of small objects that might bring forth a variety of associations. You should have at least one for every student in your class. These objects might include such things as a ruler, rubber band, string, scissors, kitchen utensil, baseball, picture frame, etc. Put these into the grocery bag.

To begin the activity, explain to students that one way to have some fun learning about oneself and each other is to randomly pick some object and then think about how something about it or what it is used for is like you.

Explain that each student will reach into the mystery bag and select one item. He or she will then tell the class how he or she feels the item is like him/her.

Proceed until all students have had a turn.

Shoe Box About Me

(Primary/Intermediate Levels)

Objective   Students will be inspired to be curious and learn more about their classmates.

Strategy   Sharing activity

Materials   Shoe boxes, paper bag, or similar

Procedure   Ask each student to find at home a shoe box, paper bag, or other similar sized closeable container. Tell the students to fill the box with things about themselves—favorite snack, pictures, favorite items, artwork they've done, etc.

Ask the students to then bring the filled shoe box to class. Have each student share with the group what he or she put into the box and why.

Variation

If you know how to get in touch with your students before the school year begins, you might consider sending them a letter asking them to bring to class on the first day a bag with 8–10 special items that say something important about themselves. You may wish to make suggestions as to what sorts of things to include, such as something they collect, a magazine picture of their favorite sport, the best book they've ever read, an award they've received, or something in their favorite color.

On the first day of class, ask students to use their bags to help introduce themselves.

Map of Me

(Intermediate Level)

Objective   Students will be encouraged towards self-disclosure through a non-threatening activity.

Strategy   Drawing activity

Materials   Large pieces of drawing paper, marking pens or crayons

Procedure   Give each student a piece of drawing paper. Tell them that they are to think of themselves as a place. What they will now do is to draw a map of what they would look like as that place. They might choose to see themselves as an island, a city, a country, or some imaginary land. Whatever they choose, they should draw in the kinds of buildings, roads, mountains, lakes, etc., that represent how they would look as this place.

When students are finished, let each student describe to the group the place he or she has drawn, explaining more about his or her choices of what was drawn. The pictures can then be put up around the classroom.

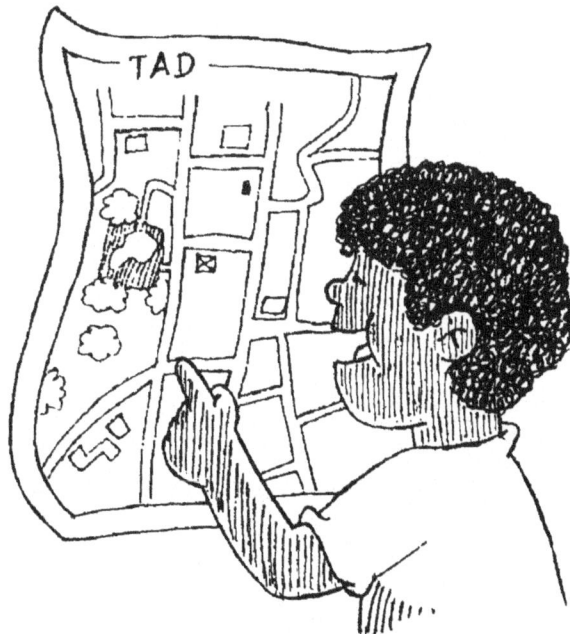

Who I've Been

(Intermediate Level)

Objective   Students will develop an increased awareness of each other.

Strategy   Guessing game

Materials   Baby pictures supplied by students, paper, tape or glue, pencils or pens

Procedure   Ask your students to bring from home pictures of themselves as a baby or very young child (if they can't obtain a picture, they may draw one of themselves as a baby). Students are not to show this picture to other students. In class, ask students to attach these pictures to a sheet of paper and then write a few clues below it that might help other students guess who is in the picture. Put these up around the room. Beneath each picture put a blank sheet where other students can record their guesses as to who each photo is. Students then individually go from picture to picture writing down their guesses.

Interviewing a Classmate

(Primary/Intermediate Levels)

Objective   Students will become acquainted with each other at the beginning of the school year.

Strategy   Interviewing activity in pairs

Materials   Interview Guide as stated below, or use handout (following)

Procedure   Interviews are an excellent means for students to become better acquainted with each other. This activity will often foster new friendships and feelings of self-importance. When students don't know their peers, they tend to make assumptions and develop unfounded biases. As students interview each other, they learn new information that promotes diversified friendship patterns in the classroom.

You may wish to introduce the interviewing process by creating an interview guide. To do this, you list or have your students list 10 questions that would help them know a classmate better.

Following are three possible approaches:

1. Write the questions on the chalkboard and tell each student to choose a person whom they do not know very well and, using the questions as a guide, learn as much as they can about their partner. If students don't come up with enough appropriate questions, use those you like from the list. After five minutes, ask each student to share the information about his or her partner with the rest of the class. Because you are a group member, you should participate in this activity, too.

2. Another approach to interviewing also begins by developing a list of questions students might ask each other. These are written on the board and referred to as students interview each other in pairs. After these questions have been asked, each pair of students joins with another pair. The four students share the new information they have learned about their partners. After a few minutes, ask the class to reconvene and each person to share three things about his or her partner with the class.

3. Still another choice is to make the guide into a handout. Divide the students into pairs and give each student this interview guide handout. Each student then interviews his or her partner

and writes the answers on the interview guide. When students have completed their interviews, have each student introduce his or her partner by saying, "This is _____. Two interesting things I learned about him or her are _____ and _____." When they are done, ask the partner if the information given was accurate.

For all approaches, finish the interview process by asking the group of students what interesting things they learned, what they discovered they have in common with someone else, how it felt to be interviewed or to be the interviewer.

Variation

Students can come up with their own interview questions by using the five words "who," "what," "where," "why," and "when." This helps them avoid asking questions with "yes" or "no" answers, which yield little information to an interviewer.

Sample Interview Guide

What is your name? _____

Do you have any brothers or sisters? _____

What do you like to do most? _____

What do you hate to do? _____

What is your favorite book? _____

What is your favorite TV program? _____

What is your favorite school subject? _____

What is your hardest school subject? _____

Do you have any pets? _____

What sports do you like? _____

What was fun about your summer vacation? _____

What is the most interesting place you have ever
visited? _____

What are your favorite hobbies or activities? _____

The Interview Whip

(Primary/Intermediate Levels)

Objective Students will become acquainted with one another.

Strategy Interview activity—fast questions

Materials None

Procedure This approach is similar to a personal interview, except that the pace is much faster. You ask a student a question. After that student answers, you ask another student the same question and then another, and so on. Select questions from those that follow or make up your own.

1. What's one thing that bugs you?

2. What is the best thing you have bought with money you have earned yourself?

3. What is your favorite flavor of ice cream?

4. What kind of pet would you like to have?

5. Where would you like to go on a trip?

6. What is your favorite TV commercial?

7. What's the title of the last movie you saw?

8. What's one thing you like to do after school with a friend?

At the conclusion of the session, you might have a class discussion centering around these questions: What are some of the similarities or differences you noticed? What are some things you learned about others in the class?

The Interview Chain

(Primary Level)

Objective	Students will become acquainted with one another.
Strategy	Interviewing activity—group.
Materials	None
Procedure	This approach is similar to a personal interview. You ask a student a question. When it is answered, that student gets to ask another student a question of his or her choice or from your suggestions. The chain continues in this manner.

It may be helpful to have some sample questions on the board so that the pace of questioning moves rapidly. Some possible questions follow, or you may make up your own.

1. What's your favorite food?

2. If you could be someone else in history, movies, books, sports, etc., who would you be?

3. Where's your favorite place to go on a weekend?

4. What's your favorite dessert?

5. What's your favorite sport?

6. What's your favorite school subject?

7. What's your favorite holiday besides Christmas or Hanukkah?

8. What kinds of pets do you have?

9. What do you usually do at home after school?

Have a class discussion centering around these questions:

• What are some of our similarities and differences?

• What are some of the things you learned about one another?

Public Interview

(Primary/Intermediate Levels)

Objective   Students will become better acquainted with one another.

Strategy   Interviewing activity—two-way

Materials   None

Procedure   Tell your class that you will be conducting interviews as a way of helping them become better acquainted with one another. Describe the procedures as follows: Volunteers will come to the front of the room. You will ask questions about the student's life following a typical talk-show format. (It is recommended that you not ask questions on personal belief systems or private matters.)

The rules are:

1. The student always has the option of passing if he prefers not to answer a question.

2. The student may end the interview at any time by simply stating, "Thank you for this interview."

Some sample questions are:

1. If you could be any age, what age would you like to be? Why?

2. Did you go on vacation this year? If you could go anywhere in the world you wanted to next year, were would you go?

3. What are some things you like to do? What do you hope to be able to do in the future?

4. What do you like best about school? Least?

5. If you were a teacher, what would you like to teach? Why?

6. What changes would you make to improve this school?

7. What is one of the best things that ever happened to you?

8. What's your favorite food? Why?

9. What's your favorite dessert? Why?

10. If you could be any animal, what would you be? Why?

11. What's your favorite sports team? What do you like about it?

12. If you could be anyone you wanted, who would you be?

13. If you could have any job in the world, what would you pick?

14. What would you most like to get as a present?

15. If you could be really good at something, what would it be?

16. What is your favorite recording group or artist? Why?

17. Do you have any pets? What's an interesting fact or story about one of them?

18. What is your idea of a perfect Saturday afternoon?

19. What is the best news that you could get right now?

20. What is one of your best accomplishments?

21. What is your favorite place nearby to eat?

22. What are two things that really bug you?

23. What is one of the most unusual articles in your home?

24. Who is the most memorable person in your life? Why?

25. What is the worst toy you've every owned? Why?

26. Where is the strangest place you've been? What was so strange about it?

A final interviewing approach has several students serve as reporters. They interview their peers and obtain such information as: where students were born; the number of members in their family; a student's favorite television show, food, color, or animal; a special hobby or pet; any unusual places they have traveled to; and students' future goals. The information is tabulated and can either be duplicated and given to each student or you can make a large chart on the wall for other classes to read.

Information Exchange

(Primary/Intermediate Levels)

Objective   Students will get to know a student better by asking him questions.

Strategy   Interviewing activity—pairs

Materials   None

Procedure   Divide students into pairs. Set a time limit of 3 to 5 minutes and have one student in each pair tell his partner as much as possible about himself including interests, talents, accomplishments, family life, etc. Students will then reverse roles. When time is up, they will introduce their partner to the class, giving information that they just learned in the activity. They might say, "This is _____ and this is what I learned about her."

Variation

Students can make a collage using words and pictures that depict their background, hobbies, interests, favorite things, and future goals. This collage can be explained to a partner who then presents it to the class explaining what it reveals about its maker.

Giving Your Opinion

(Intermediate Level)

Objective   Students will become better acquainted with one another.

Strategy   Interviewing activity using a poster

Materials   Interview Topic Poster, Interview Topic Envelope, paper bag

Procedure   Make an Interview Topic Poster (sample illustration on back of this page) as follows: Cut a large poster board in half. Write the interview topics (about 8) on strips of different colored construction paper. Suggested topics are listed on the sample poster on the next page or you may wish to include your own ideas. Label a manila envelope "Interview Topic Envelope" and put into it two squares of each color that you used on the poster.

Put all students' names on slips of paper in a bag. Draw one name at a time and have that student come to the front of the room. (A student may pass if he or she wishes.) The student then draws a colored square from the envelope and matches it with that color on the poster. The topic written on that colored strip becomes the topic for that student's interview. Classmates may raise their hands and ask the student for his or her opinion, ideas, and thoughts on the topic.

Special rules for this activity should include:

1. No put-downs or embarrassing questions.

2. The student being interviewed can pass on any questions he does not want to answer.

3. The student may end the interview at any time by simply saying "Thanks for the interview."

Classmates could be encouraged to recognize the efforts of the student being interviewed and applaud when he is done.

After you have used this activity for a while, you may not need the interview poster. You can simply pick a student's name and have the class interview on any and all topics.

INTERVIEW TOPICS

Hobbies/Interests	Sports
Holidays/ Celebrations	Family
	Weekend Activities
Places to Go	Smorgasbord (All Topics)
School	

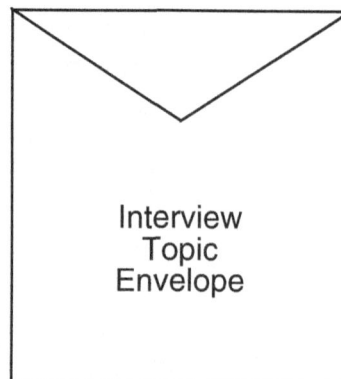

Interview
Topic
Envelope

Double Circles

(Intermediate Level)

Objective   Students will become acquainted with one another.

Strategy   Interviewing activity—one-on-one

Materials   None

Procedure   Ask for 12 students to volunteer for this circle activity. Assign six to be in the inner circle and six to be in the outer circle. Students will stand in the circles and will face a partner in the opposite circle. When students are properly positioned, tell them that the purpose of this activity is to practice getting acquainted quickly with others. Tell them that they will have one or two minutes to talk with each partner in the opposite circle. Topics they could discuss include:

1.   What do you like to do in your spare time?

2.   What places do you like to visit?

3.   Who would you like to be for a day?

4.   What's your favorite music group?

5.   What are your favorite hobbies or activities?

6.   What do you like about school?

The inner circle should rotate in a clockwise direction every one or two minutes until all students have talked with everyone in the opposite circle.

When the activity is over, group discussion could center around these questions:

1.   What did you learn about a classmate that you didn't know before?

2.   What was the most interesting thing you learned during this activity?

3. Can you remember something about each person with whom you talked?

4. What were some of the things you discovered you had in common with other students?

Getting Acquainted

(Primary/Intermediate Levels)

Objective   Students will become better acquainted with their classmates by exchanging information.

Strategy   Writing activity and/or question and answer exchange

Materials   Question list, paper, pencil

Procedure   Listed below are some questions that can be used in a variety of ways. Students could be assigned a different question each day and write in a journal. These answers could be confidential or they could be shared with other classmates if students wish. Students can work in pairs and exchange answers to questions either conversationally or by reading the answers to each other. Partners can be changed frequently so that students have a chance to get to know something about a number of people. Questions can also be answered in small groups of four to six students.

1. What was your favorite toy as a young child?

2. What were you most proud of as a young child?

3. Did you have a nickname? If so, what was it and did you like it?

4. Do you like your first name? If not, what would you like your name to be?

5. What is your favorite possession?

6. Did you once have a favorite possession you don't have now? How do you feel about no longer having it?

7. What is the funniest thing that ever happened to you?

8. What is the silliest thing you have ever done?

9. What is your all-time favorite movie?

10. What is your favorite book? Why?

11. Who in your family are you most like? In what ways?

12. If you had to be someone else, who would you be?

13. Why is your best friend such a good friend?

14. Name something you hate to do.

15. How would you change this class to make it better?

16. What kinds of pets do you have?

17. What is your favorite TV show and book?

18. What is your favorite school subject?

Getting to Know the Teacher

(Primary/Intermediate Levels)

Objective   Students will become better acquainted with their teacher.

Strategy   Talk and interviewing activity

Materials   None

Procedure   Jot down 10 or 15 things you enjoy doing. Pick three or four that stand out as most important to you and spend a few minutes simply talking with your students about your interests.

Invite your students to "interview" you so that they might come to know you better.

After sharing some of your priorities and your life with your students, put the following sentence stems on the board:

I learned that _____

I was surprised that _____

I wonder _____

Ask for volunteers to finish the statements.

If some students seem interested in sharing some of themselves with the class, as you have, let them become the focus person.

Variation

Write a letter on the chalkboard or overhead that describes you, your life outside of school, your interests, family, or pets. Invite your students to write back sharing themselves as you have done.

Silly Moves Circle

(Primary Level)

Objective   Students will get to know one another through a fun game.

Strategy   Group game

Materials   None

Procedure   This is an entertaining way to build a sense of group cohesiveness.

Ask participants to stand in a circle. The first person performs a silly action, such as making a face or hopping and spinning around backwards. The next person repeats the first person's action and then adds a new silly action of his or her own. Continue in this manner around the circle, with each person repeating the old actions and adding something new.

Move That Ball

(Primary/Intermediate Levels)

Objective   Students will become acquainted with someone in the classroom whom they don't know (or don't know very well).

Strategy   Paired activity involving moving a ball together.

Materials   Playground ball

Procedure   This activity may be done either in the classroom or outside on the playground. Divide the students into pairs and, as much as possible, put students together who do not know each other. Give each pair a ball and determine a goal for them to accomplish. For example, they could do the following: Get the ball into the wastebasket, move it under the goal post on the playground, move it a specific distance, etc. Each pair must move the ball without the use of their hands and feet. They could move the ball by placing it between their backs and walking together. Other variations might include putting the ball between their chests or their sides. Besides a playground ball, you could use a balloon, water balloon, Ping-Pong ball, marble, or beanbag.

Source: Adapted from *Relationship Builders*, by Joy Wilt and Bill Watson.

Personality Chairs

(Primary Level)

Objective   Students will engage in a physical activity that helps them get to know each other better.

Strategy   Musical chairs type of game

Materials   Chairs

Procedure   This game works like Musical Chairs except that instead of music, questions about personal characteristics are used.

Arrange chairs in a circle with one less chair than there are students. Select one student to start and have all other students take a seat.

Explain that, like Musical Chairs, the object is not to be the person left standing. Students will move in response to whether or not they fit the characteristics asked by the student who is standing. For example, if he or she says, "Who in the group likes pizza?" then everyone who likes pizza must get up and find a new seat. That new seat must be at least two seats away from their last seat.

All of the questions asked must be in the form of "Who in the group. . .?" Only those students who fit the category move, with the exception that the student asking the question always moves regardless if he or she fits the category asked.

Questions should not be too general or too specific. Questions like "Who in the group is in the fourth grade?" or "Who in the group has a white cat named Snow?" are not good questions for this game. If a student needs help formulating a question, he or she may ask the teacher for help.

Remind students before beginning to move in safe ways and never to bump or shove. Also, remind them again that the object is NOT to be the one asking the questions.

The Best of My Friend

(Intermediate Level)

Objective   Students will prepare a commercial that advertises the best qualities of their classmates.

Strategy   Discussion, drawing

Materials   The "Best of My Friend" handout (following); construction paper, felt tip pens, or crayons; roller movie theater

Procedure   This activity is excellent at the beginning of the school year.

Have students work in pairs interviewing one another using copies of the handout that follows. Discuss techniques of TV commercials emphasizing the importance of creating a commercial that will appeal to an audience. Tell students to create a commercial that will show interesting things about their classmate and would make others want to know him. The commercial can be shown to the class in a roller movie format. Have students use 4 or 5 sheets of 12" x 18" construction paper, putting pictures and words on each sheet of paper to depict a special quality about their classmate. The sheets can then be taped together and mounted on the roller movie. Students can, one at a time, "sell" their classmate to the audience by showing the advertisement and reading the words.

Directions for creating a roller movie theater:

You will construct a movie theater similar to the one illustrated on the back of this page. Take a cardboard box and cut a rectangular shape out of it slightly smaller in size than the 12" x 18" sheets of construction paper used for the "commercials." Cut holes on the sides of the box at both the top and bottom, as shown in the illustration. Next, insert wooden dowels. Students will tape one end of their commercial to one dowel and the other end to the second dowel, rolling it up so that the first picture is in view in the opening.

Source: Adapted from *Miraculous Me*, by C. Nickersch, C. Lollis, and E. Porter.

Variation

If you choose not to do this activity at the beginning of the year as a means of helping students get to know each other better, then change the format slightly. Instead of having students interview their classmates, arrange for them to go into another class of the same grade and interview students there.

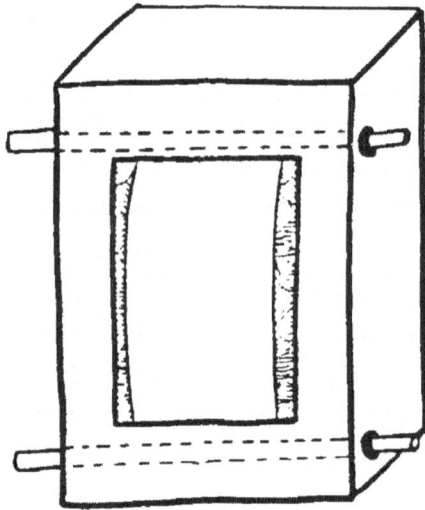

The Best of My Friend

Name _____

1. In school what subject do you like best and why?

    _____

2. What sports and hobbies do you like?

    _____

3. What are some things you help do at home?

    _____

4. Tell about a time you were proud of something you did.

    _____

5. What are some things you do in your free time.

    _____

6. What special things do you own?

    _____

7. Tell about something you plan to be successful at someday.

    _____

Section B

Climate-Building Activities

List of Climate-Building Activities

Introduction

Each of the activities in this section is designed to help students:

- Feel that they are important and respected members of the classroom group.

- Become caring and responsive to their classmates.

The activities involve the use of a wide variety of procedures. These procedures have all been tried many times and have been found effective in establishing a positive learning environment. Some procedures are designed to be used for a few minutes each day, some once per week, others monthly or only once during the school year.

It is recommended that you glance through the activities and earmark those you feel are in line with your teaching style and belief system. You might then choose one or more to implement right away, making a note to yourself regarding others you would like to use at a later date.

Secret Pals

Objective   The students will show consideration for others and make new friends.

Strategy   Group activity

Materials   The "Secret Pals" handout (following), names of students written or typed on slips of paper

Procedure   Type the names of your students, cut up this list, fold each slip twice, and have students draw names for their "Secret Pal." (At some grade levels, boys prefer to draw only from boys' names and girls from girls' names.) It is easier to keep the "secret" if students don't tell other classmates who they draw. During the following weeks after the drawing, students can provide surprises for their Secret Pal in any number of ways. Here are some suggestions.

1.   They can write notes complimenting their Secret Pal on something positive they observed him or her doing. They can write clues as to who they are. (They should disguise their handwriting or have another student write their notes for them.)

2.   They can make up crossword puzzles or other games to put into little booklets for their Secret Pals.

3.   They can give small gifts, such as something from home that they are tired of and would like to share with someone else. (All gifts must have an attached note saying something positive, and be signed "Your Secret Pal.")

A fun activity that students can do for their Secret Pal is "a gift of a wish." Ask students to close their eyes and think about their Secret Pal. Ask them to think about what they like to do and write a special wish for that person in the form of a letter. Students may also wish to draw pictures on the letter.

The Secret Pal notes, surprises, etc. may be

1. placed in the student's desk,

2. delivered by the teacher or a friend, or

3. placed in a set of "mailboxes" (milk cartons, shoe boxes, paper towel tubes, or file folders provided by the teacher for this activity).

Students may write thank you notes to their Secret Pals and place them in their mailboxes. These thank you notes are then picked up by the Secret Pals as they deliver something. You may also choose to set some space aside on a blackboard where students may write little thank you notes with chalk to their Secret Pals or tape notes onto the board.

You are to decide the length of time before students reveal their identity to their Secret Pals. On the day you select, students should be asked to try to guess who their Secret Pals are. If they guess correctly, they are then asked to tell what clues they used or how they found out. (This helps students avoid being detected next time.) If they don't have any idea who their Secret Pal is or guess incorrectly, the teacher says, "Will the real Secret Pal of _____ please stand up?"

Comments: Students often like to have another name drawing after the revealing of Secret Pals. If they draw the name of the person they just had, they may put that name back and draw again. This should be the only reason for re-drawing. The point of the activity is to be able to show thoughtfulness and kindness to anyone.

A good time to reveal the names of Secret Pals is at special holidays during the year, such as Halloween, Valentine's Day, St. Patrick's Day, etc. This makes school events or parties on that day even more festive.

To: Patty,
From: Your Secret Pal

I just wanted to let you know that . . .

Thank You Notes to Secret Pals

April 9
Dear Secret Pal,
I want to tell
you how much I
appreciated . . .

Dear Secret Pal,
The surprise
you left in my
desk . . .

Secret Pals

I did lots of things as a Secret Pal this week. Listed below are some of them.

1. _____

2. _____

3. _____

4. _____

5. _____

6. _____

7. _____

8. _____

Listed below are some of the things my Secret Pal did for me.

1. _____

2. _____

3. _____

4. _____

5. _____

6. _____

7. _____

8. _____

Student of the Week

Objective Students will have an opportunity to share some of their special interests with their classmates.

Strategy Bulletin board features student

Materials Bulletin board materials

Procedure Construct a "Student of the Week" bulletin board. Use the following format or one of your own.

Student of the Week

Name: _____

Favorite: Photographs

TV show _____
Person _____
Animal _____
Sport _____
Food _____
Game_____
Place _____

This bulletin board can be used repeatedly if students fill out cards and staple them to the appropriate place on the board. Instead of writing out their "favorites," students could use drawings to illustrate them.

To begin the program, draw names of two students. The first one drawn will be the student of the week for the next week of school, the second one drawn will be student of the week for the week after that. Alternately, you may choose the student of the week by alphabetical order or by selecting the first student of the week and having him or her choose the next week's, etc. Whichever method, select a name at the end of each week, so that students have plenty of time to prepare their bulletin board.

Explain to students that the week they are the special person in the room is a good time to bring their hobbies and special interests to school to display for their classmates. This is an opportunity for each student to tell others about his or her hobbies and/or interests, and to answer questions about them. The student of the week should also be given various classroom privileges. NOTE: With younger students it is a good idea to send a note home to the parents asking them to help gather photographs, hobbies, etc.

Monday is a good time for the student of the week bulletin board to be put up. If possible, spend a few minutes with the student to help him plan his display. Then he can go over his display with the class and explain his favorites, photographs, hobbies, etc. On Fridays you may have a writing activity called "A Story About the Student of the Week." Students will write a short story or perhaps draw a picture about the special person. The student of the week draws a cover for a book to contain these stories about him written by his classmates. Remind students that their story should mention the strengths of the student and certainly no put-downs. Before going home, the student of the week should take down his display so that the bulletin board will be ready for the next week's special student.

Friday Forum

Objective   Students will reflect upon the past week and respond to select questions.

Strategy   Writing, group discussion

Materials   Paper, pencils

Procedure   Each Friday, choose a few questions like the ones listed below and write them on the board. Ask students to write on one or more of the topics and hand their papers in. Explain that their ideas and opinions might be beneficial to the class and that, while you will not reveal who wrote a certain response, you would like to share some responses with the class. Have students make a star by any response they don't want shared with the group.

Sample Friday Forum Questions:

1. The best thing about this week was . . .

2. I didn't like it when . . .

3. I was disappointed when . . .

4. I improved in . . .

5. I'm having trouble in . . .

6. The way I felt about being part of this class was . . .

7. I wish . . .

8. I wish our class could . . .

9. I want to know why . . .

10. I wish I had . . .

11. Compared to last week, this week was . . .

12. Next week could be better if . . .

Change the questions each week, if desired. It takes only a few to elicit good responses.

Variation

Set aside a special time each week for students to voice what's on their minds. Let them express complaints, give compliments, discuss problems, ask questions, or make announcements.

Daily Comfort and Caring

Objective   Students will express some of their concerns at the beginning of the school day so that they can better give their attention to school subjects.

Strategy   Brainstorming-style discussion

Materials   None

Procedure   At the beginning of each day, gather the class together. Take a few minutes to explore with students their feelings or physical needs, either of which could be a potential block to the day's learning. Often these blocks can be dispelled just by talking, especially if someone is there to listen. This is a time to help students with simple problems and worries like a forgotten lunch, a sick pet, or losing a pencil. It is a time to listen caringly to the student who may not have slept well, or another who is being hassled by older kids at the bus stop. Explain, however, to students that it is not appropriate to discuss serious problems that involve home or relatives and family, as family members may consider it an invasion of privacy. (These can be discussed with the teacher privately, if necessary.) This is also a time for students to share exciting things that may be occurring in their lives so that, having shared them, they can better focus on academic tasks. With this in mind, questions to open up discussion might include these:

- Does anyone have any problems to take care of before we start working?

- Is anyone concerned or excited about something that will keep him from concentrating?

- Before we start the day's work, do any of you have something on your mind that you would like to take care of?

Thumbs Up, Thumbs Down

Objective   Students will have an opportunity to determine and to express their feelings about a topic or situation, and to be alert to the feelings of others.

Strategy   Quick question and answer

Materials   None

Procedure   Explain to your students that thumbs up is a positive (+) sign and a negative (-) expression is thumbs down. A wiggly thumb indicates that you aren't sure of your reaction to a given question.

Then say to the class that periodically you will check on how they feel about things by saying, "Show me thumbs up or thumbs down." Demonstrate how this will work by asking, "Are you happy today? Show me thumbs up or thumbs down."

You may ask further questions (some examples are listed below) at this time to reinforce the concept. Thereafter, either on a regular or intermittent schedule, use the "thumbs up, thumbs down" activity.

This activity has many applications and is a quick way to gain an expression or reaction. Students should be encouraged to observe other classmates' reactions to these questions. This activity is an effective way to gain the attention of the class. It also allows the teacher to get in touch with his or her students on a variety of topics.

Sample Questions:

- "Are you happy today?"

- "Do you feel peppy today?"

- "Did you have/will you have a good weekend?"

- "Has someone hurt you today by something they said?"

- "Are you proud of yourself today?"

- "Did you have a good breakfast today?"

Focusing on the Positive

Objective   Students will identify what is negative about tattling and replace it by making positive comments about one another.

Strategy   Group activity, circle discussion

Materials   None

Procedure   Point out that at times students try to get each other in trouble by tattling. Ask students if they will turn this unkind behavior around and tell something good about someone instead of something negative. For instance, for young children suggest a "tattle-good" session where students tell about the good things they have noticed someone do. Model this behavior by giving an example: "I have a tattled-good on Johnny—he helped me carry something today."

Another simple, but effective, counter to a pattern of being negative about self or others is to end the period or day with a "positive circle." Here the students and teacher each tell something new and good that has happened since the last class, a high point in their day or week, or something they did that they are proud of—in other words, something each person feels really good about. When finished, everyone then says something appreciative or admiring about the person on his right (or left), round-robin style, so that each person also receives a positive comment. (The statement can involve a personal trait, something someone has done, or something attractive about a person.)

NOTE: Students may feel silly or giggle during this exercise. They need to be made aware that the purpose of these circles is to make themselves and others feel good, and the laughter is like a put-down. Once the habit of paying attention to people's good strengths and qualities becomes established, the ability to praise comes more easily and everyone's self-esteem grows.

The Rights We Have in This Classroom

Objective   Students will realize that each class member has the same rights and will be treated with respect.

Strategy   Group discussion

Materials   The "Rights We Have In This Classroom" sign (following)

Procedure   Read through "The Rights We Have in This Classroom" and discuss each section. Explain that each person in the class has these rights and that you will see that they are enforced. Post the sign where students can see it. On occasion, remind students of their rights and resulting responsibilities to one another.

The Rights We Have in This Classroom

I have a right to be treated with kindness in this room.
  This means that no one will laugh at me, tease or
  insult me.

I have a right to be myself in this room.
  This means that no one will treat me unfairly because
  I am fat or thin, fast or slow, boy or girl.

I have a right to be safe in this room.
  This means that no one will threaten me, bully me,
  push me or destroy my property.

I have a right to be heard in this room.
  This means that no one will yell or shout, and my
  opinions will be considered in any plans we make.

I have a right to learn about myself in this room.
  This means that I will be free to express my feelings
  and opinions without being interrupted or criticized.

The Class Council

Objective   Students will respond appropriately to choices for leadership in the group. Students feel more responsibility for what occurs in the classroom.

Strategy   Group discussion, meetings, and representatives council

Materials   None

Procedure   Either select or have the class select four members to form a class council. Boys and girls should be equally represented. Council members should elect a chairman from among themselves. These students will "serve" for a certain length of time, usually two weeks. All students should have the opportunity to be on the council before anyone gets a second turn.

The council can aid in decision-making involving such things as the games to play at recess, arrangement of furniture in the room, planning of a class party, and the establishing of classroom rules, procedures, and routines. It is suggested the council begin with nondisciplinary issues and, as communication skills increase, progress to more difficult issues.

Set aside a specific and regular time for council meetings. Spontaneous meetings may also be called as the need arises. Sitting in a circle is desirable, but not necessary. An agenda should be displayed in a prominent place where students can add to it, but let them know that not all items will always be covered. End the meetings before students become bored and restless (approximately 10–20 minutes). Remind class members to deal with each other with mutual respect and that the nature of the meeting is to help each other. Review the minutes before the next meeting.

The council can also serve as a grievance committee, but it should be made very clear that the council's purpose is one of defining issues and making recommendations rather than handing down decisions and making out punishments.

For complaints, any student may make a complaint against any other student or group, but it should be in writing. This forces the student to greater thought and effort before making a complaint.

The council makes its recommendations after hearing both sides of a complaint. The recommendation should stress what should be done in the future by both parties to avoid repetition of the complaint. While the matter of assessing blame cannot be completely avoided, the primary purpose of the council in handling grievances should be to aid in understanding and prevention rather than set blame and determining punishment.

In all cases, the final decision of what action, if any, is to be taken rests with the teacher.

Student Attitude Questionnaires

Objective   Students will anonymously share some of their thoughts and feelings about classroom life.

Strategy   Writing activity, group discussion.

Materials   Questionnaire #1—"Perception of Teacher Questionnaire"
Questionnaire #2—"Sharing Your Thoughts and Feelings About School"
Questionnaire #3—"Report Card for the Teacher"
Questionnaire #4—"How Am I Doing?"

Procedure   One way to help children feel that their thoughts and feelings are valuable is to listen to them and find out, quite specifically, what they have on their minds. The systematic gathering of data from students allows teachers to make educational changes that will increase learning. Additionally, gathering information from children that does lead to changes clearly says to children that their feelings and thoughts count.

The questionnaire "Sharing Your Thoughts and Feelings About School" provides a method for you to gather valuable information from your students. It can be filled out anonymously. Students should understand that honest information is helpful to you and that you will receive it in a completely nonjudgmental way. In addition to using the questions suggested, you may wish to make up items that relate directly to whatever you wish to discover. Just tell your students you would like their help in becoming a better teacher.

A useful way to deal with the data generated by the questionnaire is to hold meetings with the class to discuss the results. Again, it is essential to be accepting and open, rather than defensive. The attitude "What are some things I (or we) can do about that?" goes a long way toward establishing the kind of classroom climate that you feel good about.

Sources: *Children's Interviews,* by N. Miller; and "Report Cards for Teachers," by E. Hunter, in *Childhood Education.*

The questionnaires "Report Card for the Teacher" and "Perception of Teacher Questionnaire" can help you in your professional growth. Again, the questionnaires need not be threatening nor should the results be particularly painful if you realize that no one is perfect in all things and that people grow in stages, generally by focusing on one area at a time for improvement.

(No name, please.)   Date _____

Perception of Teacher Questionnaire

The statements below tell some ways students might feel about their teacher. "Score" each statement to show how you feel.	Never	Not very often	Usually	Always
1. He/she respects me.	1	2	3	4
2. He/she tries to see things the way I do and understands how I feel.	1	2	3	4
3. He/she pretends to like me more than he/she really does.	1	2	3	4
4. He/she doesn't seem to like me very much.	1	2	3	4
5. He/she tells me her opinions more than I want to know them.	1	2	3	4
6. He/she is interested in knowing how I feel about things.	1	2	3	4
7. It seemed to bother him/her when I talk or ask about certain things.	1	2	3	4
8. He/she likes seeing me.	1	2	3	4
9. He/she understands me.	1	2	3	4
10. I feel I can trust him or her.	1	2	3	4
11. He/she just tolerates or "puts up with" me.	1	2	3	4
12. There are times when I think that what he/she says does not show what he/she really feels.	1	2	3	4
13. He/she hurries me when I ask for help.	1	2	3	4
14. I often feel he/she has more important things to do when I am talking to him or her.	1	2	3	4
15. Even when I can't say what I mean clearly, he/she still seems to understand me.	1	2	3	4

(No name, please.)   Date _____

Sharing Your Thoughts and Feelings About School

1. What do you think is really good (worthwhile, important, great) about YOU? ____

   _____

2. What's something about yourself you would like to change? _____

   _____

3. What are some things that teachers in your school do to help you feel good about
   yourself? _____

   _____

4. What are some things that teachers in your school do that make you feel not so
   good about yourself? _____

5. What are some things that people in your family do that help you feel good? ____

   _____

6. What are some reasons why grownups should care about (be nice to, respect)
   children? _____

   _____

7. If you could talk to all the grownups in the world, what would you say to them
   about how they should treat children? _____

   _____

8. Are there some things that other kids do in school that you don't do? What are
   those things? _____

9. What are some things that you have to do that other kids don't do? _____

   _____

10. What do you like to do best in the classroom? Tell me one thing.

    _____

11. What does your teacher like to do best? _____

    _____

12. When is your teacher the happiest? _____

    _____

13. Is it ever hard for you to ask the teachers the questions you have?

_____

14. If yes, what makes it hard to ask questions? _____

15. What are some ways the teacher helps you? _____

16. What are some other things the teachers could do to help you? _____

_____

17. Is there something you would like to do in school that you haven't done yet? ____

_____

18. Is there something that you would like to learn or know more about?

_____

19. Do you usually work with other children or by yourself? _____

20. Are there times when it's hard to work because of other children? When is it
    hard? _____

21. What would you like the teacher to stop doing?

_____

_____

22. What would you like for the teacher to start doing that he/she doesn't do now?

_____

_____

23. Do you have a favorite place in your classroom? Where? _____

24. Is your classroom different from other rooms you've had before? How is it
    different? _____

25. How would you like to make your classroom different? _____

_____

26. Are there times when you don't want to come to school? If yes, what are those
    reasons? _____

_____

27. When you're in school, what is the best part of the day for you? _____

_____

(No name, please.)   Date _____

Report Card for the Teacher

Rate your teacher on this scale by placing the appropriate number in the parenthesis after each question.

1 - Always
2 - Almost Always
3 - Occasionally
4 - Almost Never
5 - Never

1. My teacher tells me when I do a good job. ( )

2. My teacher tells my class when we do well. ( )

3. My teacher lets each member of my class handle different types of responsibilities. ( )

4. My teacher has a "bossy" tone of voice. ( )

5. I feel I can discuss problems with my teacher. ( )

6. My teacher "picks" on certain class members more than others. ( )

7. My teacher lets us work together and cooperate with our friends. ( )

8. My teacher tries to get everyone to be part of the class activities. ( )

9. My teacher treats some class members better than others. ( )

10. My classmates and I are allowed to express our own opinions. ( )

11. My teacher likes to try new ideas. ( )

12. Most students in my class like our teacher. ( )

13. My teacher makes all the decisions for the class. ( )

14. All students get a chance to talk and express opinions. ( )

15. My teacher understands the problems of children our age. ( )

16. My class "picks" on certain students. ( )

17. My teacher feels the same about many problems as most class members do. ( )

Source: *Giving Kids a Piece of the Action,* by A. Smith, J. Cooper, and M. Leverte.

(No name, please.)   Date _____

How Am I Doing?

	Always	Usually	Seldom	Never
1. I give clear directions.				
2. I give a reasonable amount of homework.				
3. I give you extra help if you need it.				
4. I understand your problems.				
5. I listen to you when you want to talk.				
6. I let you express your opinions.				
7. I am polite.				
8. I discipline fairly.				
9. I admit when I am wrong.				
10. I listen to your suggestions.				
11. I am friendly.				
12. I make school interesting.				
13. I am a good sport.				
14. I care about your feelings.				
15. I treat you fairly.				
16. I know what's going on in the room.				
17. I am patient.				
18. I have a good sense of humor.				
19. I am honest.				
20. I am organized.				

Suggestions for ways I could be a better teacher.

_____

_____

Celebrating Birthdays

Objective   Students will acknowledge one another on their birthdays.

Strategy   Writing exercise, group-completed book

Materials   Papers to form a book or plain 3" x 5" cards, paper crown (optional)

Procedure   On birthdays (or assigned "un-birthdays" for those with summer dates), students write stories or comments honoring the birthday person such as:

"I like _____ because . . ."
"_____ is nice because . . ."
"_____ is my friend because . . ."
"_____ is a neat guy/girl because . . ."

These can be illustrated with pictures and can either be signed or given anonymously. They are then collected, made into a book (or, if cards were used, put in a stack) and handed to the birthday person. Students enjoy receiving these special notes and should be encouraged to reread them, especially on days when they're feeling a bit "down" or discouraged.

The following are some other ways to celebrate students' birthdays:

- Make a birthday crown that the student may take off the shelf and wear only on his or her birthday.

- Tape an "Our Birthday Person" sign to the birthday child's chair or tie a balloon to the desk.

- Allow students to bring treats on their birthdays to share with their classmates.

- Have classmates make a group card for the birthday friend. Fold a piece of construction paper in half. Have one or two students design an appropriate cover. Pass the card around the room and encourage students to sign it and make brief comments.

- Allow the "birthday child" to skip every other question or problem on an assignment or give some other such special privilege.

- For summer birthday students, you may wish to have the students make cards that you can give to the child's parents. They can then give these to the student during the summer on his or her birthday.

Don't forget to celebrate the arrival of a new baby brother or sister or other special event in the life of a student, too.

Open House

Objective   Students will engage in creative activities in preparation for an Open House.

Strategy   Art or writing activities

Materials   Poster board or tag board, shirt or jacket, crayons, old newspapers, camera, special projects on display

Procedure   Special activities for Open House focus on the individual child:

1. On the poster board students draw a life-size head with neck and shoulders of themselves, coloring both sides. They bring shirts or jackets from home to put around the back of the chair. The head, with the neck inside the clothing, is then taped to the chair. If the sleeves are long, stuff them with newspaper and prop them on the desk to give the appearance of a student writing. Hands that fit inside the long sleeves may be added, and can be made to appear as if they are holding a pencil or opening a book.

2. Students write a "letter" to their parent(s) or caregivers, emphasizing their best qualities as a mom and/or dad. They may leave them on the desk for parent(s) to find at Open House.

3. Special projects by the children, reflecting their best work, should be on display.

4. Get samples of each child's work—a different assignment for each child so there is no comparison—and attach a picture of him/her working at the desk.

5. If you had students complete the ASSIST "I'm One-Of-A Kind" workbook from *Building Self-Esteem in the Classroom*, you may wish to have them leave these on their desks for parents to look at.

6. If you have access to the ASSIST manual *Building Self-Esteem in the Classroom*, you may want to have students do some or all of the following Supplementary Art Activities: Self-Portrait, The Story Of My Life, Coat-of-Arms, Creative Names, My Name and Me, My Own Collage. Display their work for Open House. Some ideas may also be found in the Supplementary Writing Activities such as What's in a Name?, The Daily News, 'Wanted' Poster and Write a Cinquain.

Chain of Friends

Objective   Students will recognize the importance of their contribution to the class.

Strategy   Art activity

Materials   1-1/2" x 14" strips of paper in different colors, crayons, magazines, glitter, paper clips

Procedure   Ask students to choose a strip of paper in a color they like and decorate it with pictures, drawings, glitter, etc. Each student should write his name on his strip of paper, along with one or two words describing some of his special interests or skills.

When everyone is finished, interlock the strips in a chain and fasten them together. This may be done with glue in a permanent way or with paper clips or tape in such a way that any one link could be taken apart again.

Display the chain in the classroom. If the detachable version of the chain is made, the link representing a particular child may be taken off when he is absent from class, showing a break in the chain.

Discussion could focus on the following question: "All the links are different, but they make up a complete and unique chain. What happens to our chain when a link is missing?"

Graffiti Mural

Objective   Students will express their ideas freely on a variety of topics.

Strategy   Writing activity

Materials   Large piece of construction paper or tag board, colored markers

Procedure   A graffiti mural is a non-threatening way for students to express their ideas and feelings. It also allows them to expand on the ideas of other students. A large piece of paper placed on a section of a chalkboard or wall can be used for the mural. A table can also be used by covering it with paper. Put a sentence starter or "title" at the top of the mural. For example:

> "School is . . ."
> "Students are . . ."
> "Friendship is . . .
> "I like teachers who . . ."
> "To improve this classroom, I would like for our class to have . . ."
> "It's tough being a kid because . . ."

You may need to provide encouragement for students to express themselves freely. You might wish to express your "teacher opinion" when the mural is completed. A few basic ground rules might be that

1) everyone contributes at least once, and

2) nothing may be written that makes fun of another person.

After most students have contributed is a good time for a class discussion focusing on the topic of the mural.

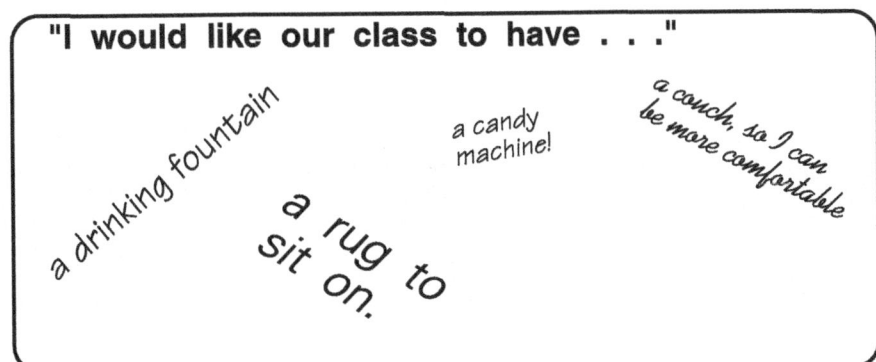

"I would like our class to have . . ."

a drinking fountain

a candy machine!

a couch, so I can be more comfortable

a rug to sit on.

"Dear Abby" Mail Bag

Objective   Students will explore their own skills as problem solvers.

Strategy   Letter-writing, group discussion

Materials   Paper, pencils, large grocery bag

Procedure   Bring several relevant "Dear Abby" columns from the newspaper and read them to the class. Students could also bring some they think are interesting and pertinent to them.

Ask students if Abby's answers sound practical and realistic or, if not, what they would have said instead.

Place a large grocery bag with "Dear Abby Mail Bag" written on both sides at the front of the class. Have the class write letters to "Dear Abby" about typical problems that come up in the daily routine of classroom life and sign them with anonymous pen names.

Read through the letters and select those that would be useful for class discussion. Read the letters chosen to the class and ask students what advice they would give the writer.

A Writing Bulletin Board

Objective   Students will share their written work with one another.

Strategy   Bulletin board activity

Materials   Bulletin board supplies

Procedure   A writing display may be something you and your class wish to use as a part of the room decorations for the entire year. The outlines of each student made during this activity can stay up indefinitely.

Each student should draw an outline of himself or herself and print his or her name on the clothing. Some students may wish to show themselves carrying small signs with their names on them. Writing efforts of each student can be added from time to time. Students should be allowed to choose which efforts they wish to have displayed. Samples of creative efforts would be great to display for Open House, etc.

Students can add seasonal ideas to the big wall group picture. Pumpkins, Christmas themes, valentines, birthday wishes, etc., are just a few of the alterations that can be made. When the school year has passed, the students can take down their outlines and see if they have grown. They may then write stories about how it feels to grow for a year. Christmas stories and poems can be added during the holiday season. At Valentine's Day, each student can write a Valentine message to the class and tape it on his outline.

If each outline contains a fake pocket, students can be encouraged to write notes and letters to each other. Instead of passing them during class, notes can be placed in the appropriate pocket, and as each student leaves for home, he or she can pass by his or her outline and collect what has been written. This would be a convenient place for the teacher to leave messages. Be sure your outline is up on the wall along with those of your students.

Source: *The Good Apple Creative Writing Book.*

Personalized Math Story Problems

Objective   Personal information about students will be integrated into math problems, allowing students to learn about each other as they learn math.

Strategy   Math story problems

Materials   None

Procedure   Using information from previous get-acquainted activities, compose story problems that relate to specific students and their interests. An example might be: "Susan likes to roller skate. She also likes the color blue. Roller skating costs $1.00 for each hour of skating. To rent blue roller skates costs 50¢ for each hour. If Susan skates for two hours, how much will she spend?"

You might let older students create their own story problems. These can be made into an assignment book. Students might also illustrate their story problems if you wish. Copy these and distribute them to the class.

Variation

There is no reason this personalizing technique cannot be applied to other areas as well. Students can be encouraged to use their interests and awareness to add a special "slant" to history ("What would it feel like to explore the unknown woods? Johnny, you like to hike—what do you think?"), or science ("Lucinda likes to collect rocks. She can be one team leader in this assignment. Who else likes rocks?"), or other subjects.

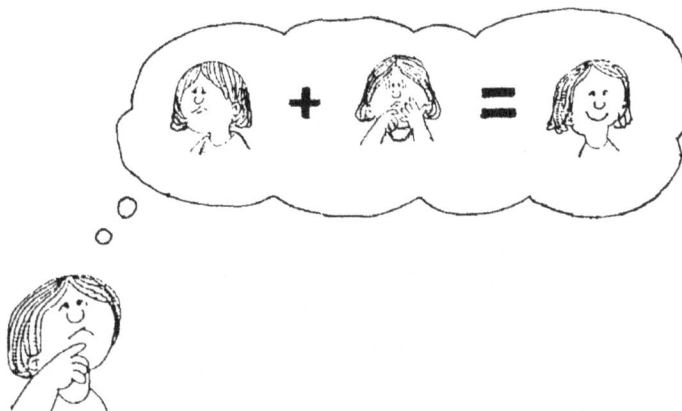

Class Spirit

Objective   To promote increased cooperation, enthusiasm, and communication among class members and the feeling of pride in the classroom.

Strategy   Bulletin board

Materials   Note cards, bulletin board, class picture or individual pictures (optional)

Procedure   A Class Spirit bulletin board can begin when a compliment or positive statement is made about your class. For example, when one of your colleagues mentions that your class was especially courteous during a school assembly program. Share this comment with your class, then write it on a card and tack it to the bulletin board. If a visitor comments on the attractive art work in your classroom, report the comment, then add it to the bulletin board. A substitute teacher might remark about the cooperation given to her by your class during your absence. This comment, too, could be recorded and added to the Class Spirit bulletin board.

Children enjoy the positive comments made by others, and they tend to pull together to earn more of them. They are eager to share the bulletin board with their parents and other visitors to the classroom. Children tend to check the board at regular intervals to read what has been added. Most important, however, is that the children become aware of the teacher's attention to the things they do well. Such awareness builds positive feelings between the teacher and children.

Another way to build class spirit is to have students decide on a special class name. They might also make an emblem, select a motto, and choose class colors. These can be used on the outside of the classroom door, for classroom displays, and on messages to parents and students. Using many of the same techniques as athletic teams helps a class develop a "team" spirit. This same approach can be done by each cooperation group in your class if you use cooperative learning groups or "tribes."

Cross-Age Helpers

Objective   Students will experience positive feelings about themselves through the process of helping others.

Strategy   Tutoring by students

Materials   Variable, determined by the academic task

Procedure   Cross-age helpers are typically two to three grade levels ahead of the children whom they tutor. These helpers provide extra classroom assistance and help build the self-esteem of the children with whom they work.

Children profit a great deal from cross-age tutoring and rapport usually quickly develops between the two children. Invariably, the younger child looks up to his or her older friend.

The task of cross-age helpers is to reinforce skills that have already been presented. It is helpful to teach the helpers game techniques to use during their tutoring sessions. Arrange regular talks with the tutors. Remember to praise them, answer any questions they have, discuss any problems they are having and give them constructive suggestions for future sessions. Students who have academic problems themselves seem to thrive on cross-age tutoring. They enjoy going to a primary classroom and having students practice reading to them or to a kindergarten where they teach simple skills (e.g., P.E., skipping, jumping rope, etc.).

Source: *Self-Esteem: A Classroom Affair*, by M. Barba and C. Barba.

Hobby Show

Objective   Students will become aware of the uniqueness of themselves and each other and to take pride in something they do well.

Strategy   Display of hobbies or collections for students from other classrooms to view

Materials   Each individual student will develop whatever materials are needed for his/her display (see below).

Procedure   Have a discussion about what hobbies or collections students have that they could display. Explain to students that hobbies can be "interests" or collections. A student who has an interest in skiing or the Civil War, for example, can use this interest for his or her display.

Show students library books about things people collect like coins, stamps, doll furniture, etc.

Have students identify one special hobby they would like to share with others.

Have each student prepare a display for his/her desk that will explain or show off that hobby. The displays may include collections, single objects, pictures, drawings, or almost anything a desk will hold.

Invite other classrooms to come to the room to view the displays. Students should stand by their own desks to explain their hobbies and to answer questions.

Student Newspaper

Objective   To help students write about their achievements and activities and to share these with their families.

Strategy   Writing activity

Materials   Paper, pens and pencils, and a method of reproducing your class newspaper (ditto, copier, etc.)

Procedure   Articles and features are to be written and compiled by class members every month. Articles could include class activities, compliments the class received, examples of good work, new things that were learned, areas of study, etc. Each student should have the opportunity to have something "published" during the year. Editions can be taken home and shared with students' families. The name for the paper should be decided upon by the students. Students can also provide artwork or graphics.

Catch Them With a Camera

Objective   Students will feel positively reinforced when they see a photograph of themselves engaged in an activity.

Strategy   Photography combined with various activities

Materials   Camera, film (you may wish to consider an instant picture camera)

Procedure   The use of a camera in the classroom can be an interesting and exciting way to focus on the strengths of children. Children like to have their pictures taken. A picture is truly worth a thousand words when it communicates to a child that he/she is important and valued.

At times, let the children take pictures, too. Every child can experience a feeling of success as he or she sees pictures he or she has taken of classmates, a class play, artwork, or anything that he or she may want pictured.

Pictures of children can personalize the classroom. One technique is to start out the school year by having every child's picture taken (an excellent opportunity for everyone to have a turn at being a photographer). Their pictures are then mounted on a bulletin board and each child writes something interesting about himself to place near his or her picture. Starting the school year this way is a great way to get to know the class.

Some other uses of pictures in the classroom include:

- Making duty assignments by posting the child's picture beside the duty he or she is to assume for the week.

- Using a photograph for the Student of the Week bulletin board.

- Posting pictures with articles about special events on a Class News bulletin board. The child who has a new baby brother at home could take a picture and post an announcement on the bulletin board. Photographs add authenticity and appeal to a class news board.

• Having children identify their artwork by using their photograph.

Let Them Know They Are Missed

Objective   Students who are absent will continue to feel part of the class. Students who are present will become more aware of the needs of others.

Strategy   Writing activity

Materials   Paper on which to write note, pencils

Procedure   When a student is ill or misses class for other reasons, a note or postcard from the class is a valuable gesture. Students can write a brief, cheery note. In addition to its thoughtfulness, it tells absent students that they are part of "our class" and are missed. The note may be sent home with a student who lives near the one who is absent.

Some teachers have a paper chain hanging in the classroom with each student's name on a link. When a student is absent they undo that link to show that each link in the chain is important to keep the chain together.

Welcome!

Objective   Students will plan a friendly welcome for the arrival of a new student.

Strategy   Role-play

Materials   None

Procedure   First, practice how to respond to a new student by a class role-play session. Divide the class into groups of four or more. Ask each group to select someone to play the role of the new student and someone to be the recorder of responses for the worksheet. The "new students" will leave the group. Each group should then plan a welcome for their "new student." This plan may include tours of the classroom and school grounds, as well as introductions to key staff members and other students. Then ask the "new students" to return to groups so the group can role-play their welcome.

After the role-playing, ask each new student to tell how his welcome felt. As the class devise a list of things that are important to remember when welcoming a new student. Be sure to include such things as assigning a specific "buddy" to eat lunch with the new student and the same or another "buddy" to spend recesses with the new student. Arrange for the new student to get a tour of the school and to be introduced to key school staff members. Make sure the new student gets an explanation of school rules and schedules. Schedule a time for someone to interview the new student using some of the questions in Section A of this manual, and then to introduce the new student to the class sharing some of the interview information. One fun question to ask the new student to describe the differences between his/her old school and his/her new school.

Hi! We're your welcoming committee.

Next, form an official Welcoming Committee. Rotate members monthly. After a new student has been in class for a few days, classmates can make a "wishbook" and give it to the newcomer. Each student can write about or draw something they wish for the new student. This is a wonderful way to make a new student feel welcome.

Smile Contest

Objective   Students will become more aware of smiling and being cheerful through reminders and encouragement.

Strategy   Contest

Materials   Boxes or bags, paper and pencils, posters (optional)

Procedure   Explain to your students that during this week everyone will be involved in a set of contests about smiling. Take a few moments to talk to students about how good it feels to receive a warm smile, and how by smiling we make our surroundings a friendlier place where it is easier to get along and to get to know each other.

Now tell them about the contest. Each day of this week the students will be voting on who is "best" in three smile categories. Choose the categories from the list below, and also use those as examples for students to contribute categories of their own. When you have your categories for the week, pick three to begin with today. Write these three on pieces of paper and attach these to three sacks, small boxes, or other such containers.

Students will now vote on their favorite for each category. They will write their choices on slips of paper and put them into the appropriate bag or box. Later in the day, tally the votes and announce the winners. (You may instead choose to announce the winners just before the next day's new categories and balloting.)

The handout following is a special Smile Award certificate that you may hand out to your winners or post in a conspicuous place of honor in the room.

Sample categories are:

cutest smile
widest smile
best school staff smile
friendliest smile
happiest smile
most smiles in a day

most teeth missing smile
shiniest braces smile
best singing star smile
most trustworthy smile
goofiest smile of an adult
most surprisingly nice smile

CERTIFICATE OF AWARD SMILE CONTEST

This certifies that _____

was awarded winner in the _____ *category.*

_____
TEACHER

_____
GRADE

_____
DATE

The Great Bubble Gum Machine

Objective   Students will increase positive classroom behavior and work towards a common goal.

Strategy   Rewarding positive classroom behavior

Materials   "The Great Bubble Gum Machine" picture, colored markers

Procedure   Post the picture where it can be seen by all students. Establish types of positive classroom behaviors. These might include things like coming in quietly after recess, a quick and quiet transition from one activity to another, or anything you may wish the class to improve upon and you want to reinforce.

Whenever one of the established behaviors has taken place, randomly color in a ball on the picture. Decide with the class what type of reward activity they would like when all balls are colored in. Reward ideas might include a popcorn party, a skating party after school, extra recess time, etc.

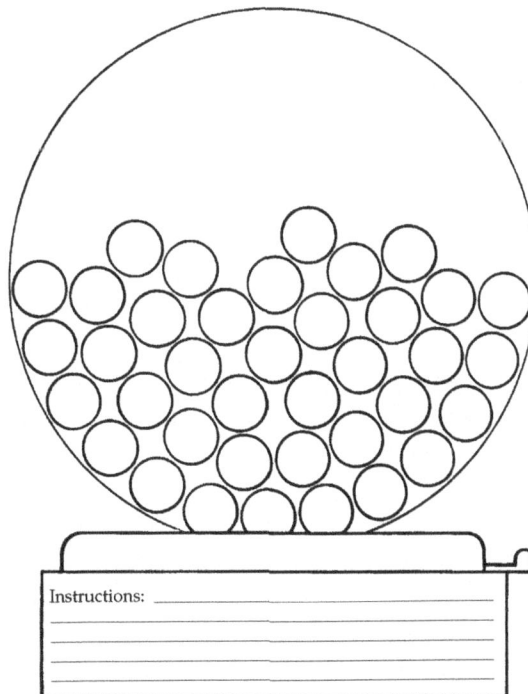

The Great BUBBLE GUM Machine

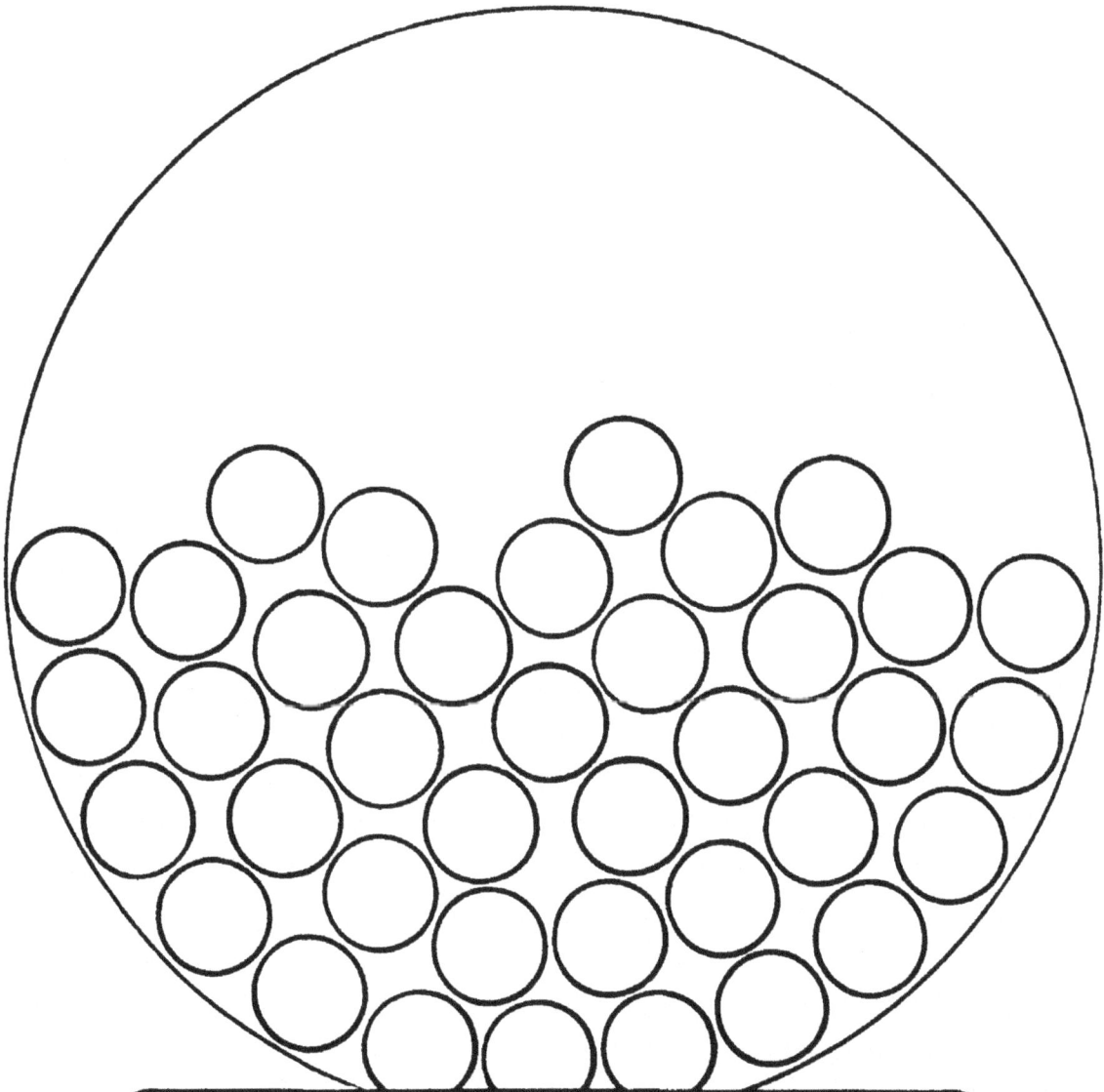

Instructions: _____
_____
_____
_____
_____

Treasure Box

Objective   Students will exhibit positive behavior in the classroom.

Strategy   Rewarding positive behavior

Materials   Two cardboard boxes (one to hold the treasures and one to hold the tickets), goodies for the Treasure Box (marking pens, sugarless gum or candy, notepads, pencils, records, models, secondhand items students donate), wrapping paper for the Treasure Box (newspaper's comic pages work fine), 1" x 2" pieces of tagboard or construction paper to be used as tickets.

Procedure   Wrap suitable "treasures" and put them inside the Treasure Box. Next, wrap the box itself. Put a slot in the top of a second box and use it for depositing tickets. On Monday morning show the students the Treasure Box, but don't reveal the contents. Tell the students what behavior they need to exhibit in order to earn raffle tickets. Remind them that the more tickets they have in the box, the better their chances will be to win the drawing on Friday afternoon. As students receive tickets during the week, have them put their names on them and drop them in the ticket box.

A benefit of this procedure is that you can give tickets for any behavior you are working on and you may give away as many tickets as you want. Tickets provide an instant reward that is quiet and nondisruptive to the normal flow of instruction.

Good for
ONE CHANCE

ONE CHANCE

Student _____

Teacher _____

Good for
ONE CHANCE

ONE CHANCE

Student _____

Teacher _____

Good for
ONE CHANCE

ONE CHANCE

Student _____

Teacher _____

Good for
ONE CHANCE

ONE CHANCE

Student _____

Teacher _____

Good for
ONE CHANCE

ONE CHANCE

Student _____

Teacher _____

Good for
ONE CHANCE

ONE CHANCE

Student _____

Teacher _____

Good for
ONE CHANCE

ONE CHANCE

Student _____

Teacher _____

Good for
ONE CHANCE

ONE CHANCE

Student _____

Teacher _____

Up and Down Bag

Objective   Students will be aware of and be rewarded for positive behaviors.

Strategy   Feedback and group reward

Materials   Paper bag, string, or twine

Procedure   Fill a paper bag with appropriate student treats or other rewards. You may also choose an all-class reward instead. Decorate the bag if you wish.

Next, attach a string to the top of the bag. Run this string over a ceiling hook or similar item, so that by pulling on the string you can raise the bag to the ceiling.

Explain to students that the bag contains a mystery treat for each of them (or for the whole class). When you see students doing the positive control or staying on-task), you will raise the bag a little. If you see the opposite, negative behavior, you will lower the bag a little. When the bag reaches the ceiling, it will be opened and the mystery treats given out.

The bag serves as a constant reminder and monitor to students of their actions. It can be much more effective to silently lower the bag than to give repeated admonitions about poor behavior choices.

Double or Nothing

Objective   Students will be rewarded for positive behaviors.

Strategy   Reinforcing positive behavior

Materials   Raffle tickets available at costume and decoration supply stores, one dice, raffle box, miscellaneous treats

Procedure   Tell students that when they are on task you will, at random times, place raffle tickets on their desks. They are to sign these and place them in a raffle box at designated times during the day. Also explain that at certain times during the day you will say "freeze." If everyone "freezes" immediately and there are no student names on the board for misbehavior, a student will be selected to roll one dice. If a one comes up, one raffle ticket with a student's name on it is pulled from the raffle box. That student will get a piece of candy or some sort of treat or privilege. If a two comes up, two raffle tickets are pulled and both students receive a reward. If a three comes up, three students receive a treat. If a four or five come up, no tickets are pulled from the raffle box. If a six comes up, everyone in the class receives a reward such as a piece of candy or a privilege such as a shortened assignment, regardless of whether they have raffle tickets in the raffle box.

This activity helps students work hard to avoid getting their name on the board for misbehavior, encourages them to stay on task, and teaches them to "freeze" when you want everyone's attention.

Award Letters and Reinforcing Notes

Awards can be used to give students recognition for such things as completion of a project; success on a test; completion of a contract; helpful contributions during class discussions; or any social, emotional, or academic progress.

Some teachers issue awards or positive notes on a regular basis, such as on a particular day of the week or month. Others issue them spontaneously, whenever they feel that a student needs or deserves recognition. One helpful procedure is to write an award or a positive note to one student each day after school and take it to the student's desk. By checking off student names on the class list as you give them awards, you can be sure that everyone receives recognition at one time or another for something they do well in the classroom. If you have a child who tends to have difficulty earning recognition in any way, try to adjust the expected outcome in some area so that the child can be successful in at least one thing and thus legitimately earn an award.

You may wish to use some of the awards and positive notes from the following pages to acknowledge student effort and achievement. After students have completed all of the ASSIST units (see *Building Self-Esteem in the Classroom*, *Teaching Friendship Skills*, *Helping Kids Handle Anger*, *Teaching Cooperation Skills*), you may wish to give them the ASSIST diploma.

Super Student Award

Presented to _____

For _____

_____
Keep up the good work!

Signed _____

Certificate of Award

To _____

Because _____

_____

_____

Date _____

Signature _____

Happy Gram

You _____

_____

_____

_____

_____

Signature _____

I Thought Today Was ☑

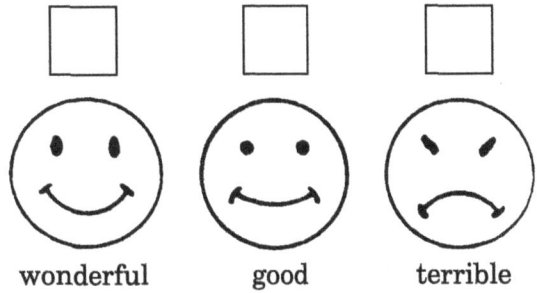

wonderful   good   terrible

because . . . _____

_____

_____

_____

_____

I Am Proud to Say You

_____

_____

_____

_____

_____

Signature _____

You _____

_____

_____

_____

_____

Signature _____

Super Attitude

To _____

About _____

_____

_____

_____

A Compliment to You

_____

_____

_____

_____

_____

_____

_____

_____

Super!!

_____

_____

_____

_____

_____

_____

_____

TERRIFIC

_____

_____

_____

_____

_____

_____

_____

Section C

Individual Behavior Improvement Plan

Introduction

In any given classroom a number of behavior problems arise during the school day that can make it difficult to maintain a positive classroom climate. The ASSIST Individual Behavior Improvement Plan provides the teacher with a plan for solving typical classroom behavior problems.

In dealing with inappropriate classroom behavior, it's important to avoid the "putting out behavioral fires" mode. It's more effective to think in terms of prevention. This can be accomplished by having goals for student behavior and prioritizing these goals.

The first step in prevention is to identify the students whose classroom behavior is interfering with their own or others' academic learning and to establish specific social or behavioral goals for these students. After that, when a problem involving these students occurs, you will be able to respond according to established priorities. You will have determined which of these students' behaviors should be encouraged and reinforced, and which behaviors should be ignored for the time being.

While students with the worst behavior problems are clearly the ones who first need your help in setting behavioral goals and achieving them, it's important to also think about the needs of other students as the year goes on. Quiet or shy students often have needs as urgent as those of any of their peers. These students should eventually have a goal to work toward in the same way that disruptive students do. Additionally, students who have already achieved basic behavioral goals should be helped to establish other affective goals that might broaden their outlook, improve their attitudes or help them develop new personal/social skills. By looking at the Personal/Social Behavior Inventory, you and a student can determine any number of goals that would be valuable to work towards.

After the worst behavior problems in the class have been eliminated, a good procedure would be to help one or two students each week select a goal and set up a behavior improvement plan. This way you will be helping each student in your classroom make some affective growth or positive behavior change over the course of the school year.

While some students will require your time and attention to achieve their goal, others will be able to work toward their goals with little active involvement from you.

Formulating a Behavior Improvement Plan

The ASSIST Individual Behavior Improvement Plan involves a series of steps designed to resolve individual behavior problems and to strengthen appropriate classroom behavior. Go through the following steps either by yourself or in conference with the student:

1. Either fill out or review the Personal/Social Behavior Inventory. This inventory offers a comprehensive listing of behaviors whereby you can obtain a profile of a student's personal/social behavior. From this profile you will be able to pinpoint specific areas that need remediation and to identify goals and behavioral

objectives to facilitate affective growth. These can be written as behavioral objectives for an Individual Education Plan (IEP) for special education students. (See "Developing an Affective Individual Education Program [IEP] for Special Education Students Directions" later in this section.)

2. Identify either an inappropriate behavior to be decreased or an appropriate behavior to be encouraged, or both.

3. Determine a plan of reinforcement to help the student achieve and maintain the new behavior. (See "A Reinforcement Menu" later in this section.)

4. Decide how often the behavior must occur to earn the reinforcement. (You should make the reward easily obtainable at first.)

5. Develop the content of an explicit contract between teacher and student. (See "Student-Teacher Contract" later in this section.)

If you haven't involved the student yet in the planning of the program, do the following at this point:

6. Show the student the Personal/Social Behavior Inventory, pointing out some traits you identified as strengths and some traits you identified as needing improvement, and explain your reasons for these ratings.

7. Summarize the behavior improvement plan, including reinforcement strategies, that you will be using, and ask the student for suggestions regarding changes or additions.

Now that the student understands the program and the reasons for using it, encourage his/her active participation in the following ways:

8. Together, fill out the Student-Teacher Contract and sign in the appropriate places.

9. Review together the Student-Teacher Discussion Sheet regarding the behavior improvement plan.

10. Determine if the student really knows how to perform the new behavior. Most students need to see the behavior modeled, practice it a few times, and receive feedback before they are able to do it on their own. (See "Teaching Personal/Social Skills Directions" later in this section.)

11. Ask the student to count each day the behavior that is the focus of concern, and enter the count on either the Behavior Improvement Chart or the Weekly Progress Chart. (See both later in this section).

12. Be consistent in initialing the student's count column at the end of the day and in giving positive reinforcement.

13. Ask the student for advice and suggestions for changing the procedure when his/her Behavior Improvement Chart indicates that a change is needed. If no improvement occurs after two weeks, change the reinforcer.

14. Remember that teaching and maintaining appropriate social behavior is an ongoing process. Maintenance of the target behavior will occur more often if you ignore inappropriate behavior and respond positively to appropriate behavior when it is demonstrated by the student. Let students know you are interested in and supportive of their efforts.

Below is a list of materials provided that have been designed to help you implement the Individual Behavior Improvement Plan:

1. Personal/Social Behavior Inventory

2. Student-Teacher Discussion Sheet

3. Behavior Improvement Chart

4. A Reinforcement Menu

5. Student-Teacher Contract

6. Weekly Progress Chart

7. Teaching Personal/Social Skills Directions

8. Developing an Affective Individual Education Program (IEP) for Special Education Students Directions

9. Flow Chart for Affective Individual Education Program (IEP) for Special Education Students

Personal/Social Behavior Inventory

The scale consists of major categories of affective behavior equated on two ends of a continuum. In order to retain the sensitivity of the scale in describing the range of behaviors, the indicators listed under each major category include both specific behaviors and interpretations of behaviors. Between each two categories are the numbers:

-3   -2   -1   +1   +2   +3

Decide which of the two categories describes the student better and circle one of the three numbers next to that word as follows:

1.   a little more on this side

2.   definitely on this side

3.   very much on this side

As much as possible, base your ratings on outward behavior you actually observe.

Determine with the student some specific goals and objectives that would facilitate movement towards the appropriate behavior in the areas selected for focus of concern.

You may wish to circle the appropriate descriptive words to make your inventory more specific.

Personal/Social Behavior Inventory

SELF-CONCEPT

Name _____

Teacher _____

School _____

Date _____

INAPPROPRIATE BEHAVIORS

1. **Body language demonstrates low self-confidence**
   poor eye contact; poor posture, bites nails, frowns

2. **Overly critical of self**
   degrades physical self, and/or work; rejects compliments; poor grooming; views self as ineffective

3. **Adapts poorly to new situations, activity or group**
   refuses to participate; develops physical complaints

APPROPRIATE BEHAVIORS

1. **Body language demonstrates self-confidence**
   good eye contact; good posture; smiles; looks happy

2. **Indicates positive feeling regarding self**
   accepts compliments; refers to self in positive terms; accepts physical limitations; good grooming; demonstrates pride in accomplishments and possessions; feels capable

3. **Easily adapts to new situation, activity or group**
   willing to try; participates in new endeavors and challenges

Date	very much on this side	definitely on this side	a little more on this side		a little more on this side	definitely on this side	very much on this side
	-3	-2	-1		+1	+2	+3

Personal/Social Behavior Inventory

SELF-CONCEPT

Name _____ Teacher _____ School _____ Date _____

	INAPPROPRIATE BEHAVIORS		APPROPRIATE BEHAVIORS	

Date	very much on this side	definitely on this side	a little more on this side	a little more on this side	definitely on this side	very much on this side
	-3	-2	-1	+1	+2	+3

4. **Inappropriately submissive or passive** — overly complying; easily intimidated; seeks constant reassurance; overly controlled verbal and non-verbal behavior; inhibited

4. **Appropriately assertive** — expresses own ideas, feelings and needs; seeks help when appropriate; expresses opinions, even when contrary to opinions of others

Date	very much on this side	definitely on this side	a little more on this side	a little more on this side	definitely on this side	very much on this side
	-3	-2	-1	+1	+2	+3

5. **Excessively upset by mistakes/failures/criticism** — gives up; blames others; pouts; is defensive; gives rationalizations or excuses; overreacts to or denies criticism; easily hurt

5. **Copes with mistakes/failures/criticism** — re-attempts; continues work on a difficult task until it is completed; learns from mistakes and criticism; accepts and evaluates criticism

Date	very much on this side	definitely on this side	a little more on this side	a little more on this side	definitely on this side	very much on this side
	-3	-2	-1	+1	+2	+3

6. **Low tolerance of conflict and/or antagonism** — cannot cope with being teased; withdraws from conflict; feelings easily hurt

6. **Tolerance to conflict and/or antagonism** — sees conflict as resolvable; feelings stable; responds to teasing by ignoring or other constructive means

Personal/Social Behavior Inventory

SELF-CONCEPT

Name _____ Teacher _____ School _____ Date _____

INAPPROPRIATE BEHAVIORS		very much on this side	definitely on this side	a little more on this side		a little more on this side	definitely on this side	very much on this side		APPROPRIATE BEHAVIORS
		-3	-2	-1		+1	+2	+3		
7. **Unrealistic appraisal of self and competencies** over/under emphasizes personal strengths; over/under emphasizes personal weaknesses; self expectations too high/low	Date									7. **Realistic self-appraisal** deals appropriately with personal strengths and weaknesses; sets appropriate expectations

Personal/Social Behavior Inventory

INTERPERSONAL RELATIONSHIPS

Name _____

Teacher _____

School _____

Date _____

	INAPPROPRIATE BEHAVIORS		APPROPRIATE BEHAVIORS

1. Poor emotional control
emotional outbursts; hits; fights; pushes; uses put-downs; makes inappropriate remarks or gestures; pouts; whines; does not wait for turn

1. Good emotional control
even tempered; expresses anger with nonaggressive words; talks to others in a tone of voice appropriate to the situation; walks away from peer when angry to avoid hitting; smiles when meets acquaintances; waits for turn

	very much on this side	definitely on this side	a little more on this side		a little more on this side	definitely on this side	very much on this side
Date	-3	-2	-1		+1	+2	+3

2. Physically avoids social contacts
shuns others; isolates self; hides; runs away

2. Appropriate social interactions
accepting; friendly; joins others; responds to social overtures; helps peer when asked; initiates conversation with peers; asks another student to play on the playground

Date	-3	-2	-1		+1	+2	+3

3. Withdraws from classroom activities
inattentive; detached, indifferent; rarely speaks; listless; apathetic; just sits; daydreams

3. Participates in classroom activities
attentive; involved; responsive; asks to be included in group activities in progress; participates in class discussion

Date	-3	-2	-1		+1	+2	+3

Personal/Social Behavior Inventory

INTERPERSONAL RELATIONSHIPS

Name _____

Teacher _____   School _____   Date _____

INAPPROPRIATE BEHAVIORS							APPROPRIATE BEHAVIORS
	very much on this side	definitely on this side	a little more on this side	a little more on this side	definitely on this side	very much on this side	
4. Rejects expressions of appreciation and affection seeks no close relationships; doesn't keep friends; demonstrates lack of trust; suspicious	Date −3	−2	−1	+1	+2	+3	**4. Gives and receives expressions of appreciation and affection** reacts positively to friendly overtures; seeks close relationships; makes and keeps friends; trusts others appropriately; gives sincere compliments
5. Inappropriate leadership behavior bullies, bosses others; tries to dominate; seeks to win or be first	Date −3	−2	−1	+1	+2	+3	**5. Appropriate leadership behavior** compromises; accommodates; can be in leader or member role; can work in small or large group
6. Disruptive of classroom group activities talks out; out of seat; teases; overly excitable, makes irrelevant remarks; bothers or distracts others; clowns, tattles	Date −3	−2	−1	+1	+2	+3	**6. Cooperates with others in classroom group activities** listens and contributes appropriately; stays in seat; shares materials; gives in to reasonable wishes of the group; carries out plans or decisions formulated by the group

Personal/Social Behavior Inventory

INTERPERSONAL RELATIONSHIPS

Name _____ Teacher _____ School _____ Date _____

	INAPPROPRIATE BEHAVIORS	very much on this side -3	definitely on this side -2	a little more on this side -1	a little more on this side $+1$	definitely on this side $+2$	very much on this side $+3$	APPROPRIATE BEHAVIORS	
7.	**Overly dependent on others** clings; monopolizes teacher/peer time; applies undue emotional pressure; will not make independent decisions; overly conforming; constantly trying to please; easily led							**Appropriately independent of others** works out conflicts without intervention; seeks help appropriately; does not apply undue emotional pressure; self-reliant; expresses own views	7.
8.	**Poor communication skills** poor eye contact; doesn't listen; interrupts; awkward overtures; overly talkative							**Good communication skills** good eye contact; attends; observes; responds appropriately; pays attention to the person speaking; waits for pauses in a conversation before speaking	8.
9.	**Intolerant of individual, cultural, or ethnic differences** ridicules; uses racial or cultural slurs; pokes fun; intolerant of others							**Accepts and appreciates individual cultural and ethnic differences** accepts different life styles; open minded; shows tolerance for persons with characteristics different from one's own	9.

(Each scored row labeled "Date" with columns: -3, -2, -1, $+1$, $+2$, $+3$)

Personal/Social Behavior Inventory

INTERPERSONAL RELATIONSHIPS

Name _____ Teacher _____ School _____ Date _____

INAPPROPRIATE BEHAVIORS		APPROPRIATE BEHAVIORS
10. Shows little interest in others' needs, problems or feelings		**10. Shows interest and caring regarding others' needs, problems or feelings**
does not consider others' points of view; uses others to gain; avoids helping; disregards others' feelings; impatient with or disinterested in what others say; will not apologize		considers others' points of view; reassuring; kind; comes to the defense of a peer in trouble; makes supportive comments; expresses sympathy; makes apologies when actions have infringed on rights of another; sees that others are not left out; tactful

	very much on this side	definitely on this side	a little more on this side	a little more on this side	definitely on this side	very much on this side
Date	-3	-2	-1	+1	+2	+3

Personal/Social Behavior Inventory

ACCEPTING AND HANDLING FEELINGS

Name _____ Teacher _____ School _____ Date _____

INAPPROPRIATE BEHAVIORS

1. **Does not demonstrate awareness of basic categories of feeling**
   cannot identify happiness, anger, fear and sadness

2. **Shows inability to label own feelings**
   cannot give adequate verbal description of own feeling state

3. **Exhibits lack of congruence between verbal comments and body language**
   denies obvious feeling states

APPROPRIATE BEHAVIORS

1. **Is aware of basic categories of feelings**
   can identify happiness, sadness, anger, and fear

2. **Shows ability to label own feelings**
   can make statements reporting on own feeling state

3. **Exhibits congruence between verbal comments and body language**
   verbalizes feelings that concur with observable nonverbal behavior

	very much on this side	definitely on this side	a little more on this side	a little more on this side	definitely on this side	very much on this side
Date	-3	-2	-1	+1	+2	+3

	very much on this side	definitely on this side	a little more on this side	a little more on this side	definitely on this side	very much on this side
Date	-3	-2	-1	+1	+2	+3

	very much on this side	definitely on this side	a little more on this side	a little more on this side	definitely on this side	very much on this side
Date	-3	-2	-1	+1	+2	+3

Personal/Social Behavior Inventory

ACCEPTING AND HANDLING FEELINGS

Name _____

Teacher _____   School _____   Date _____

	INAPPROPRIATE BEHAVIORS			APPROPRIATE BEHAVIORS		

4. Cannot identify feelings in others
misinterprets behavioral cues

_____
_____
_____

4. Can identify feelings in others
accurately interprets behavioral cues

_____
_____
_____

Date	very much on this side	definitely on this side	a little more on this side	a little more on this side	definitely on this side	very much on this side
	-3	-2	-1	+1	+2	+3

5. Does not accept negative feelings in self
denies fear, sadness, and anger

_____
_____
_____

5. Accepts negative, as well as positive, feelings in self
admits to fear, sadness, anger when appropriate

_____
_____
_____

Date	-3	-2	-1	+1	+2	+3

6. Expresses anger inappropriately
physically aggressive; name calls; sulks, pouts; quarrelsome; picks on others younger or weaker

_____
_____
_____

6. Expresses anger appropriately
expresses anger verbally rather than physically; directs anger toward appropriate target

_____
_____
_____

Date	-3	-2	-1	+1	+2	+3

Personal/Social Behavior Inventory

ACCEPTING AND HANDLING FEELINGS

Name _____   School _____   Teacher _____   Date _____

INAPPROPRIATE BEHAVIORS						APPROPRIATE BEHAVIORS
	very much on this side	definitely on this side	a little more on this side	a little more on this side	definitely on this side	very much on this side
Date	-3	-2	-1	+1	+2	+3

7. **Handles fear inappropriately**
denies fear; panics; refuses to engage in unfamiliar activities; clings; overly dependent; holds back

7. **Handles fear appropriately**
admits to fear; describes fear to trusted person; investigates reason for fear; willing to try unfamiliar situations that are not dangerous; has courage to face problems alone

Date	-3	-2	-1	+1	+2	+3

8. **Handles sadness inappropriately**
withdraws; condemns tears; uses sadness to gain sympathy; cries at inappropriate times and places; broods and ruminates over setbacks

8. **Expresses sadness appropriately**
shares feelings with trusted others; cries at suitable times and places; rebounds from hurt feelings

Date	-3	-2	-1	+1	+2	+3

9. **Feels uncomfortable expressing appropriate affection**
appears embarrassed or self-conscious; giggles; gushes

9. **Feels comfortable expressing appropriate affection**
gives honest compliments; makes eye contact; uses touch appropriately

Personal/Social Behavior Inventory

ACCEPTING AND HANDLING FEELINGS

Name _____

Teacher _____

School _____

Date _____

INAPPROPRIATE BEHAVIORS

10. **Responds inappropriately to feelings in others**
    insensitive; unconcerned; pursues own behavior regardless of effects on others; detached

APPROPRIATE BEHAVIORS

10. **Responds appropriately to feelings in others**
    supportive; demonstrates sympathy; adjusts behavior in ways that are thoughtful and beneficial

	very much on this side	definitely on this side	a little more on this side			a little more on this side	definitely on this side	very much on this side
Date	-3	-2	-1			+1	+2	+3

Personal/Social Behavior Inventory

RESPONSIBLE DECISION MAKING

Name _____ Teacher _____ School _____ Date _____

INAPPROPRIATE BEHAVIORS	very much on this side	definitely on this side	a little more on this side	a little more on this side	definitely on this side	very much on this side	APPROPRIATE BEHAVIORS
Date	-3	-2	-1	+1	+2	+3	

1. Does not see self as decision maker
does not demonstrate awareness that he or she has control over own behavior

1. Sees self as decision-maker
demonstrates awareness that he or she has control over own behavior

2. Does not demonstrate ability to identify alternatives
difficulty suggesting more than one alternative in a discussion; does not identify sources of help; inflexible regarding past decisions

2. Recognizes existence of more than one alternative in a given situation
can suggest more than one alternative in a discussion; identifies sources of help; can reject previous decisions

3. Does not demonstrate ability to consider consequences of actions
cannot predict consequences when asked; impulsive

3. Considers alternatives and consequences before making choice
can predict consequences when asked; patient and able to wait

Personal/Social Behavior Inventory

RESPONSIBLE DECISION MAKING

Name _____

Teacher _____

School _____

Date _____

INAPPROPRIATE BEHAVIORS		very much on this side	definitely on this side	a little more on this side	a little more on this side	definitely on this side	very much on this side		APPROPRIATE BEHAVIORS

4. Finds most decisions, including routine ones, difficult
delays; wavers; disorganized; will not make decision; overly dependent upon adults/peers

Date	-3	-2	-1	+1	+2	+3

4. Takes responsibility for routine decisions
schedules; plans; meets deadlines; trusts own judgment; initiates action

5. Avoids taking responsibility for actions
blames; makes excuses; shows "don't care" attitude; fails to do work

Date	-3	-2	-1	+1	+2	+3

5. Accepts responsibility for actions
admits errors; accepts deserved consequences of wrong doing; carries out tasks without reminders

6. Considers only self in decision-making
cannot identify who will be affected and how; insensitive

Date	-3	-2	-1	+1	+2	+3

6. Considers others in decision-making
can identify who will be affected and how

Personal/Social Behavior Inventory

RESPONSIBLE DECISION MAKING

Name _____

Teacher _____

School _____

Date _____

INAPPROPRIATE BEHAVIORS		APPROPRIATE BEHAVIORS	

7. **Does not exhibit goal setting behavior**
acts impulsively; cannot list personal goals

7. **Exhibits goal setting behavior**
establishes personal goals; makes decisions consistent with both short- and long-term goals

	very much on this side	definitely on this side	a little more on this side		a little more on this side	definitely on this side	very much on this side
Date	-3	-2	-1		+1	+2	+3

Student-Teacher Discussion Sheet

1. Goal: _____

   _____

   _____

2. What could keep me from reaching this goal?

   _____ I'm not really sure what to do.

   _____ I don't want it badly enough to work for it.

   _____ I might forget about it.

   _____ I'm afraid of what others will think.

   _____ Others don't want me to reach my goal.

   _____ The goal is too hard.

   Some other reasons might be: _____

   _____

   _____

3. What could I do so these things won't keep me from reaching my goal?

   _____

   _____

4. Who can help me?   How can they help?

   NAME

   _____   _____

   _____   _____

5. What are my chances of success?

   ☐ Very Good   ☐ Good   ☐ Fair   ☐ Poor   ☐ Very Poor

Behavior Improvement Chart

Name _____   Week of _____ to _____

Goal _____

Privilege to be gained if goal is met _____

Inappropriate Behavior	Times Inappropriate Behavior Occurred				
	M	T	W	T	F
TOTALS					

Opposite Appropriate Behavior	Times Appropriate Behavior Occurred				
	M	T	W	T	F
TOTALS					

TEACHER INITIALS					

A Reinforcement Menu

Attention and praise are usually the most powerful reinforcers. In addition to these, activity reinforcers are helpful in motivating students to try new behaviors. What is reinforcing to one student may not be to another. The best way to select a reinforcer for a student is to ask him/her what they would like to work for. If they don't know, you might offer some of the following ideas:

1. Helping in the cafeteria

2. Cleaning the erasers

3. Using colored chalk

4. Watering the plants

5. Decorating the bulletin board

6. Leading the line to recess or the lunchroom

7. Using a typewriter or computer

8. Stapling papers together

9. Feeding the fish or animals

10. Giving a message over the intercom

11. Writing and directing a play

12. Taking the class roll

13. Carrying messages to other teachers

14. Holding the door during a fire drill

15. Raising or lowering the flag

16. Distributing and collecting materials

17. Using an overhead projector

18. Operating a slide, filmstrip, or movie projector

19. Writing with a pen or colored pencils

20. Correcting papers

21. Teaching another child

22. Playing checkers, chess, Sorry, or other table games

23. Choosing a game to play

24. Being captain of a team

25. Working with clay

26. Listening to the radio with an earplug

27. Learning a magic trick

28. Being allowed to move desks

29. Sitting beside a friend

30. Going to the library

31. Helping the librarian

32. Popping corn

33. Doing a science experiment

34. Sitting next to the teacher at lunch

35. Doing crossword puzzles

36. Free time

37. Going with the teacher for pizza or an ice cream cone

38. Skipping a lesson or homework assignment

39. Doing every other item on assignment

40. Positive notes sent home

41. Special award sheets or certificates

42. Listening to records

43. Going on errands

44. Reading comic books

45. Listening to own voice on tape recorder

46. Stickers

47. Modeling with clay or putty

48. Watching filmstrips

49. Free reading

50. Listening to music with headphones

51. Puzzles

52. A favorite craft

53. Animal picture stamps

54. A reach into the "surprise box" to draw something

55. Drawing on the chalkboard

56. Playing hangman

57. Blowing up balloons and popping them

58. Playing the piano

59. Playing Simon Says or Follow the Leader

60. Working with students in lower grade levels

61. Being a line leader

62. Putting up a bulletin board

63. Extra P.E.

64. Taking a classroom pet home for the weekend

65. Getting free talking time

66. Sitting in the teacher's chair

67. Helping plan a party

68. Receiving play money for an auction

69. Spending time in a learning center

70. Receiving tickets for a raffle

71. Using the computer

Student–Teacher Contract

Name _____   Date _____

1. The behavior I will work on _____

   _____

   _____

2. What I am willing to do _____

   _____

   _____

3. Where and when I will do this _____

   _____

   _____

4. The amount of time I think I need to work on this behavior

   _____

   _____

                              Signed _____
                                            (Student)

- -

For the successful completion of the above, you may _____

   _____

   _____

                              Signed _____
                                            (Teacher)

Weekly Progress Chart

Name _____   Week of _____ to _____

Behavior _____

Put a mark every time you _____

	Monday	Tuesday	Wednesday	Thursday	Friday	Weekly Total
Teacher Initials						

- -

Name _____   Week of _____ to _____

Behavior _____

Put a mark every time you _____

	Monday	Tuesday	Wednesday	Thursday	Friday	Weekly Total
Teacher Initials						

Teaching Personal/Social Skills Directions

It may be that a student is so unfamiliar with a new appropriate behavior that the following steps are essential for successful completion of the improvement program.

Step 1.   Talk with the student about the behavior, relating it to events familiar to the student.

Step 2.   Outline the specific steps that make up the behavior, dividing them into as small steps as possible.

Step 3.   Have the student <u>practice</u> the behavior and encourage him to watch other children closely when performing the behavior.

Step 4.   Give feedback regarding the student's performance.

Step 5.   Encourage the student to perform the behavior and praise him when he does.

The following is an example of how the above steps might be done if you were helping a very shy student learn to make eye contact:

"Sally, I'd like to talk to you about something that you and I need to begin working on. I've noticed that you don't look at me when you and I are talking to each other. Most people look at each other when they talk to each other. They don't stare into each others' eyes the whole time, of course, but they look at each other most of the time.

"When someone doesn't look at me when I'm talking to them, I begin to think that the person isn't really interested in what we're talking about. But, if someone looks at me when we're talking to each other, then I think that they're interested in the conversation.

"I'd like you to try looking at other people when they are talking to you, or when you are talking to them. I do. Does that sound like something you'd be willing to work on? . . . Good.

"How about starting right now? Can you look at me? That's great. You looked at my eyes. Besides working with me on this, I'd like you to try looking at other people when they talk to you or when you talk to them. Just try it and see how it goes. Also, when you see two students talking to one another, watch the way that they look at each other. That will help you see how to do it. Wow, during the last minute or so that I've been talking, you've been watching me. That's great. I'd like you to learn to do that more often."

Developing an Affective Individual Education Program (IEP) for Special Education Students

The following format may be used by special education teachers in developing IEPs for students having deficits in the area of social skill development. The format includes a general goal statement for each area of emotional and social growth. Following each goal are examples of specific behavioral objectives. The following examples may be helpful.

GENERAL AREA: PHYSICAL CONTACT

Goal statement: The student will demonstrate positive physical contact in the classroom setting.

Objectives:
- By the end of this school year, _____ (student) will decrease by 90% the instances of negative physical contact with other students when he/she becomes angry, as measured by behavior count.

- By the end of the school year, _____ (student) will keep his/her hands to himself/herself with 90% consistency while waiting in lines, as measured by teacher observation.

GENERAL AREA: VERBAL BEHAVIOR TOWARDS ADULTS

Goal statement: The student will demonstrate the use of positive verbal interactions while communicating with adults in the classroom and in other school settings.

Objectives:
- By the end of this school year, _____ (student) will verbally respond to teacher requests in a positive manner 90% of the time, as measured by teacher observation.

- By the end of this year, _____ (student) will increase positive interactions with adults by 90%, as measured by behavior count in the school setting.

- By the end of this school year, _____ (student) will use appropriate language in verbal interactions with adults in the school setting 90% of the time, as measured by teacher observation.

GENERAL AREA: VERBAL BEHAVIOR TOWARDS PEERS

Goal statement: The student will demonstrate the use of positive verbal interactions while communicating with peers in the school setting.

Objectives:
- By the end of the school year, _____ (student) will use appropriate language with peers in the school setting 90% of the time, as measured by teacher observation.

- By the end of the school year, _____ (student) will respond to requests for information from peers using appropriate language 90% of the time, as measured by teacher observation.

- By the end of the school year, _____ (student) will decrease the number of instances of negative criticism directed towards peers by 90%, as measured by behavior count.

GENERAL AREA: NONVERBAL BEHAVIOR

Goal statement: The student will demonstrate positive nonverbal behaviors when interacting with peers and adults in the school setting.

Objectives:
- By the end of the school year, _____ (student) will smile when interacting with adults and peers in the school setting.

- By the end of the school year, _____ (student) will use appropriate physical gestures and facial expressions when interacting with adults and peers in the school setting 85% of the time, as measured by behavior count.

Flow Chart for Effective Individual Education Program (IEP) for Special Education Students

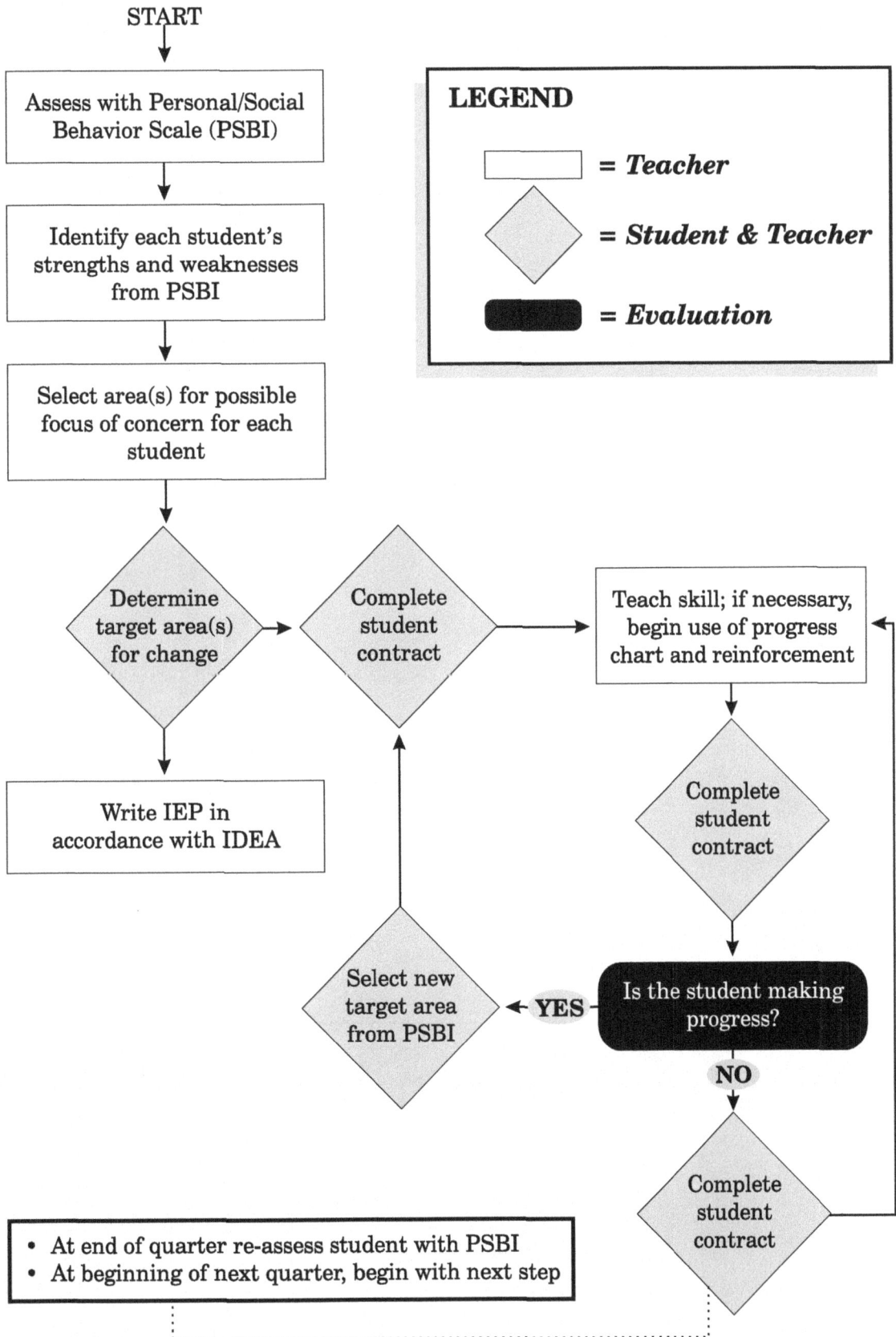

START

Assess with Personal/Social Behavior Scale (PSBI)

Identify each student's strengths and weaknesses from PSBI

Select area(s) for possible focus of concern for each student

LEGEND

☐ = *Teacher*

◇ = *Student & Teacher*

▬ = *Evaluation*

Determine target area(s) for change

Complete student contract

Teach skill; if necessary, begin use of progress chart and reinforcement

Write IEP in accordance with IDEA

Complete student contract

Select new target area from PSBI

← YES — Is the student making progress?

NO

Complete student contract

• At end of quarter re-assess student with PSBI
• At beginning of next quarter, begin with next step

Section D

Relaxation Techniques

List of Relaxation Technique Activities

Introduction

The stresses of life are inescapable. In fact, the technological developments of the last 50 years have created a world where stress can be a danger to each of us. Alarming statistics show not only a rise in the level of psychological tension and anxiety, but also a dramatic increase in stress-related diseases that were uncommon only half a century ago. Children as well as adults have unavoidable stress in their daily lives. They worry about things like lost lunches, forgotten homework, their parents divorcing, their status in their peer group, their inexperience or lack of skill in areas important to them, and a host of other things.

For some children this worry and its resulting tension are the primary contributors to headaches, stomachaches, learning problems, or disruptive classroom behavior. Tension impairs learning abilities. Many anxious children have trouble concentrating, following instructions, memorizing, organizing details, and solving problems.

To understand human functioning, learning, and behavior, it's helpful to look at the human being from a neurophysiological standpoint. A human being is, in essence, an electrical being. Humans possess a very complex set of wiring and circuits that we call the nervous system. With the proper equipment you can listen to this circuit activity. When a person is in a relaxed state, neurons fire off at a slow, steady pace. When a person is "keyed up," worried, or anxious, the firing sounds like several machine guns all going off at once. When there are large amounts of circuit activity, this interferes with the thinking process. Overactive circuits are similar to static on a radio or "snow" on a T.V. screen. When circuits quiet down again, a person is able to think more clearly, learn more readily, and act more appropriately.

Relaxing the large muscle groups of the body helps to slow down circuit activity. Teaching children to relax paves the way for a receptive attitude, stabilized mood, and increased concentration and retention, and thus leads to improved performance.

Another advantage of training students to relax is that when students learn to be more relaxed, then the classroom is more likely to be a comfortable and enriching place. Students are less likely to misbehave when they are relaxed. A relaxation exercise can also provide a good transition activity for students who have just come in from recess or who are otherwise "wound up" for one reason or another. A quick relaxation exercise helps establish a quiet, relaxed atmosphere conducive to learning.

The ability to relax is also a preventive health measure. As such, it is one of the most important skills we can possess. Some children develop the habit of holding certain muscle groups tight. They are often unaware of this until much later in life, when they may become ill or injured as a result of chronic tension. Time spent teaching students relaxation techniques can provide them with dividends for the rest of their lives.

It would be inaccurate to imply that these lessons will cause all students to develop a high degree of skill in relaxation. Whatever amount of skill students do achieve, however, will be of great use to them if they apply it. Some students may develop sufficient skill to prevent them from having tension-induced illnesses or inappropriate behaviors in later life. Other students will need more training than is possible for them to receive in the classroom to achieve this end, but even a small amount of skill is better than none.

Relaxation training can take place in any classroom setting. Once students develop the skills, they can relax themselves without instruction from the teacher and without drawing the attention of others.

A number of relaxation techniques have been developed that have been demonstrated to be effective in relaxing the body and increasing learning and performance. Presented in this section are several simplified relaxation methods based on a combination of proven techniques. These methods incorporate tensing and releasing muscles, deep breathing, and self-statements.

The first relaxation training sequence involves having students deliberately tense and then relax various muscles in the body. They do this with the muscle groups that typically become tight or tense when a person is upset or nervous. It is recommended that you try this relaxation procedure first. After two or more sessions you may wish to try the relaxation procedure in Activity 2, which involves releasing muscles without tensing them first. Then discuss with students which procedure they prefer. Use that procedure for at least four or five sessions until students know it well. Then use the abbreviated version of the same technique until students are able to use the technique by themselves without your direction. It is important for students to master one relaxation procedure before they are exposed to too many. Otherwise, they may get "overloaded" with ideas and use none of the procedures. After students learn well the relaxation technique in either Activity 1 or Activity 2, you may wish to involve them in some of the other relaxation procedures that follow these first two activities. Conclude by encouraging students to use the procedures that work best for them.

By working on any of these relaxation activities for five minutes each day, students will be able to use relaxation techniques quite naturally by the end of the school year.

After students have become familiar with several of the relaxation approaches, they may want to try making up a relaxation sequence of their own. (See Activity 6 in this section.)

Some children exhibit embarrassment or self-conscious responses when tensing and relaxing various parts of their body. They giggle or laugh as they are asked to do the procedure. Simply ignore the laughter. Remind students that this is part of the procedure great athletes and champions have learned to use, and continue. You might also praise those who are quietly following your directions.

If students misbehave during relaxation sessions, don't scold or reprimand. Instead, stop doing the exercises. Let students know that doing the relaxation exercises is a privilege, and if the privilege is abused, it is lost for that day. Explain that you'll try the exercise again the next day, but for now they are to get out their work and proceed with it.

You may find it helpful to use an audio cassette recorder to tape the relaxation scripts you use with students. As you're recording each script, use a calm, soft voice. Relaxation training is enhanced by consideration of tone, volume, and tempo. When reading the relaxation sequences, the pace at which you read should be very relaxed and leisurely. Suggest that students listen only to the sound of your voice and tune out all other sounds. You may also want them to have things on their desk tops cleared away. Some teachers like to dim the lights in the room and hang a "Please Do Not Disturb" sign on the door when they involve students in a relaxation training session.

Finally, you may find it helpful to use the taped sequence you make of one of the relaxation exercises for yourself. Teaching is such a high-pressure job and has so many frustrations, most teachers can't help but respond with some degree of muscular tension. Skill in releasing muscle tension is a key factor in job satisfaction and maintaining good health. Additionally, when you experience the benefits of relaxation, your positive attitude will be communicated to your students.

Tightening and Releasing Muscles to Relax

Objective   Students will see the value of learning to relax. Students will learn to relax by tightening, then releasing muscle groups.

Strategy   Students will participate in a teacher-directed discussion regarding the value of relaxation. (Navy pilots and top athletes have used relaxation to relieve stress and achieve peak performance.) They will then practice tightening and releasing muscle groups.

Materials   None

To the Teacher   Tensing and releasing muscles is one of the most commonly used relaxation activities. It is based on the principle that when a muscle is tightly tensed, then released, the muscle tends to feel even looser than it was before it was tightened.

To ensure that students will learn the skill of relaxation quickly and well, and that they will apply it, it's important for them to see the value of knowing how to relax. The training session begins, therefore, with an overview of some of the benefits and   applications of relaxation training.

You'll notice the words "5 seconds" and "10 seconds" in parentheses. Students should spend at least 5 seconds tensing a muscle group and 10 seconds relaxing a muscle group. This can include the time you are directing them to do this, but if your directions take less than 5 (or 10) seconds to say, you should wait a few seconds before going on to the next direction.

In teaching relaxation, as in teaching any skill, verbal praise or reinforcement should be used generously. Statements like "That really looks good"; "It really looks like you're getting the procedure down"; or "That was a nice improvement over last time," are helpful.

"Today we're going to learn some ways to relax or to loosen our muscles. It's important to know how to loosen them because when your muscles are loose, we can think more clearly and do things better."

Navy pilots needed to learn to relax   "Another thing that happens when people are under stress is that they tend to 'blow their cool' and make mistakes."

Source: Parts of this sequence have been adapted from *Relaxation*, by J.R. Cautele and J. Groden.

"A prime example of this is the fact that during World War II, U.S. Navy pilots started shooting down some of their own men."

"The military discovered that this was caused by the pilots' stress and tension."

"The Navy found that in very difficult tasks such as flying an airplane, the thing that was the greatest enemy to peak performance was tensing up."

"Tensing up can be caused by fear, lack of confidence, or trying too hard."

"In an attempt to solve this problem, the military trained some of the pilots in relaxation."

"Those who took the relaxation training course were able to identify enemy planes from their own in a fraction of a second and no longer shot down their own men."

Tensing up makes it hard to do things

Encourage students to relate this example to personal experiences they may have had where tensing up got in the way of peak performance. Then have students see for themselves that tensing interferes with performance. Have them imagine that they are taking an important test that they're really worried about. Suggest that their hands have tensed up and have them squeeze their pencils really tightly. Have them try and write a few words. Now ask them to relax their hands as much as possible and write the same words. Ask if there were any differences between the two samples of writing, and if so, what were the differences? Ask what conclusions they can derive from this activity.

Relaxation impacts sports performance

Go on to explain the following, pausing for discussion of appropriate sports performance:

"An intensive sports program was also an important part of U.S. Navy pilots' training."

"When the military was conducting the relaxation training sessions, they noticed that in the various sports the pilots were involved in, there was a marked difference in their performance here as well."

"In soccer, the pilots who had received the relaxation training became less tired, their passing became sharper, and their shots at the goal were more accurate."

"In football the halfbacks and ends could not only run faster, but could keep their speed up longer."

"The linemen found they were quicker and faster because they knew how to relax."

"Quarterbacks found they could pinpoint their throws better, and kickers could kick the ball further."

"The relaxation training seemed to have the biggest impact of all on basketball."

"After only three weeks of relaxation training, these pilots improved almost three times as much over those pilots who did not receive the training."

"They were able to steal more balls and shoot more accurately. "

"The Navy also found that in track and field tests the relaxation training helped sprinters increase their leg speed and maintain their top speed."

"Distance runners, by tensing fewer muscles, increased their strength and lowered their time."

"So what the pilots discovered was that in sports, the secret is not only to stay relaxed before an event, but to relax all the muscles not involved in performing the sport."

"This saves energy rather than wasting energy by tensing up the entire body."

"For example, what if a baseball player is up to bat? The only muscles that should be the least bit tense are the arm and shoulder muscles."

"The rest of his body should be loose and relaxed."

"Since this was discovered 50 years ago, now professional and amateur athletes in all major sports learn to use relaxation techniques to improve their coordination, speed, quickness, and endurance."

"Many top athletes feel their skill in relaxation is a key factor in their championship performance."

Relaxation impacts academic performance

Go on to explain the following:

"This wasn't all that the Navy discovered, either."

"The U.S. Navy pilots had a lot of courses and tests they had to take."

"The pilots' trainers were really surprised when the grades of those pilots who had the relaxation training shot up."

"Nobody realized that relaxation would help the pilots with their studies, too."

Relaxation impacts many other areas of human functioning

"So out of this one situation with the Navy, we learned a lot about relaxation. Now we know that when your muscles are loose and relaxed, you can do everything better; you can do school work better because it's easier to concentrate when you're relaxed."

"You can do better in sports or crafts because you can be more coordinated."

"You can use relaxation to keep from feeling nervous in a situation where you want to be 'calm, cool and collected.' " *Ask students to think of times when they don't want to appear or feel nervous.*

"Knowing how to keep your muscles loose can help you control your temper when somebody makes you mad and you don't want to blow up." *Ask students to think of times they may want to control their temper.*

"So learning to relax can help you in many ways."

"It can help you

1. learn to be calm in tense situations,

2. have more energy,

3. be able to concentrate more,

4. learn things more quickly and remember them longer,

5. do better in sports and hobbies,

6. get along with people better, and

7. have more self-confidence."

"It's a skill you'll be glad you have all your life."

Relaxation, like any skill, must be learned and practiced

"Learning to relax is like learning your multiplication tables."

"It is something that you have to practice."

"You cannot just tell yourself to relax."

"It is a skill that has to be learned through repeating it over and over."

"For the next few weeks, we will practice some of the relaxation techniques used by the Navy pilots and many great athletes."

Tensing and releasing muscles helps relax them

"A good way to learn to relax is to deliberately tense certain muscles and then relax them."

"The muscles that I'll ask you to tense are the same muscles that become tense or tight when you are upset or nervous."

"You'll learn to identify the muscles that are tight, then you'll learn to relax them."

"If you practice the things I teach you, then after a while, you'll be able to relax in a situation where you feel nervous."

You can tell your muscles what to do

"You're going to learn to have your mind tell to your muscles what to do."

"If you've never talked to your body before, it may seem a bit silly at first."

"But talking to your body helps your mind pay attention to what your body is doing."

"Let's do a simple exercise that will help you start a conversation with your body."

"Along the way it will also acquaint you with your different muscles."

"This can help you realize where tension is located in your body."

Relaxation sequence

"We'll start now."

"Sit with your back touching the chair and your feet flat on the floor."

"Put your hands in your lap. Get as comfortable as you can."

"We always close our eyes when we relax because it helps us concentrate on what we're doing and we can talk to our body more effectively."

"In addition, most people don't like others looking at them when they're learning to do something new, so tell your eyes to close so that you can concentrate on trying to learn to control your own body."

You may have to say:

"If your eyes don't want to obey you and won't stay closed, get tough with them and insist they do what you tell them."

"Good. Now that everyone's eyes are closed, we can start."

"I like the way _____'s eyes are obeying him/her."

Mention one or more students' names whose eyes are closed.

Arms and hands

"Let's start with your right arm and hand."

"Talk to the muscles in your arm and hand and tell them to grow tighter and tighter."

"Imagine that you have a whole lemon in your right hand."

"Tell your hand to squeeze it hard. Tell it to squeeze all the juice out and not leave a single drop." (5 seconds)

"Now tell your hand to relax and let go of the lemon."

"Tell your hand and arm to go completely limp."

"Notice how it feels as your hand and arm muscles loosen." *(5 seconds)*

Repeat with the left arm and hand.

Shoulders and neck

"Now we're going to tighten and relax the muscles in the shoulders and neck."

"Shrug your shoulders. Tell them to raise up and touch your ears."

"Feel your shoulder muscles tighten. Keep them tight."

"Tell your neck to tighten even more." *(5 seconds)*

"Tell your shoulders to drop down and relax."

"Tell your neck to relax, too . . . to go loose and limp."

"Notice how good it feels as the tightness goes." (10 seconds)

Chest and middle of the body

"Tell the muscles of your chest and the middle part of your body to tighten up."

"Tell all the muscles to draw in and tighten."

"Tell them to get tighter still. Feel the tension."

"Notice how uncomfortable it feels." *(5 seconds)*

"Now tell the muscles to let go."

"Let the feeling of relaxation flow through your body."

"Let your chest and middle part of your body feel limp and loose."

"Feel the relaxation spread. Notice how good it feels to be relaxed." *(10 seconds)*

Legs and feet

"Let's go now to your right leg and foot."

"Talk to the muscles in your leg and tell them to stiffen up . . ."

"Tell your right knee to lock. Tell your foot to tighten up."

"Tell your whole right leg and foot to get as tight as they can." *(5 seconds)*

"Now tell your leg and foot muscles to let go."

"Tell them to go completely loose and limp."

"Notice the pleasant feeling as your leg and foot muscles relax." (*10 seconds*)

Repeat with the left leg and foot.

Jaw

"Finally, talk to the muscles in your jaw. Tell your jaw to tighten..."

"Tell your teeth to clench. Press your tongue against the roof of your mouth."

"Feel the tension." (*5 seconds*)

"Now tell your jaw to relax . . . to go completely loose."

"Let your lips be slightly apart. Feel how good it feels to have your jaw loose and relaxed."

Breathing exercise

"Now I'd like you to take a deep breath. Hold it and then let it out."

Demonstrate by making the audible sounds that occur when taking a deep breath.

"When you breathe out, try to get your whole body relaxed from hand to toe."

"Just breathe out any tightness in your body."

"Try to imagine someone slowly waving a magic wand in front of you . . . starting at your head and slowly going down to your toes."

"Tell each muscle group in your body to relax as the wand passes each part."

"Let's do this two more times."

"I'd like you to breathe deeply again, but this time, as you breathe, I'd like you to tell your body to relax by saying the word 'Relax' to yourself."

"Drag it out slowly so that, as you reach the 'X,' you are down to your toes."

"Ready: Take a deep breath—'R-E-L-A-X.' Now you do it two more times by yourself."

Conclusion

"When you are ready, take a big stretch and open your eyes. Try to hang on to the good feeling in your body."

Ask students to describe any differences they feel now compared to before they relaxed. Point out that they have been able to make different muscle groups tense, then relax. Explain that the goal is for them to learn to check out their body often to see if any parts are tense or tight and, if so, to tell the muscles to loosen up. Say or paraphrase:

"When you scan your body and find a tense part, you can say things like 'Jaws, loosen up' Arms and hands—stay relaxed, guys,' 'Shoulders—Keep it loose!' "

"Like any other skills, the more you practice, the better you'll become."

"You should practice letting different muscles go limp several times a day."

"Especially good times to practice are when you're waiting for something or before a school, sports, or social event for which you want to be loose and relaxed."

"You can practice techniques in such a way that no one will even know what you are doing."

"Another good time to practice is when you are in bed at night."

"Practicing at night can help you get to sleep."

Tensing and Releasing Relaxation Sequence

(Abbreviated Version)

Begin

"Today we are going to do our same relaxation exercises, but this time I'm going to let you do some of it by yourselves without me guiding you."

"Here we go: Sit back in your chair and put your feet flat on the floor."

"By now you should be ready to close your eyes when we start our relaxation session."

"Good. Now that all of you have your eyes closed, let's begin."

Jaw

"Tell your jaw to tighten and your teeth to clench. Then let it relax."

"I'll wait while you do this."

Arms and hands

"Tell the muscles in your right arm and hands to tighten."

"Tighter still. Hold it. Now relax."

"Feel your arms and hands go completely loose and limp."

"Now you do your left arm and hand by yourself."

Shoulders and neck

"Tell your shoulders and neck to tighten up."

"Tighter, tighter. That's it."'

"Now let go. Feel the relaxation flow through your shoulders and neck as they completely relax."

Chest and middle of body

"Tell the muscles in the middle part of your body to tighten up."

"Every muscle should be drawn in as tightly as possible."

"Feel the tension. Good!"

"Now let it out. Notice how good it feels to just do nothing, to completely let go and relax."

Legs and feet   "Talk to the muscles in your right leg and foot."

"Tell them to stiffen up . . . tighter, tighter still."

"Now tell them to relax. Notice how good they feel, kind of warm and tingly."

"You do your left leg and foot by yourself now."

Breathing exercise   "Now take a huge, deep breath. Hold it and then let it out, saying 'relax' to yourself as you breathe out."

"Do this by yourself three times."

Students tense and release with teacher saying body part   "Now we're going to do the same thing all over again, but this time I'm going to just mention the body part and I'd like you to tighten it."

"For instance, when I say 'jaw,' tighten your jaw as best you can."

"Notice the tension and then let go and relax."

"When you're done with each part, take four deep breaths saying the word 'relax' to yourself as you breathe out."

Students tense and release without teacher help   "Now I'm going to ask you to relax each body part all by yourself, one part at a time."

"You don't need to tense them first."

"After all the parts have been relaxed, take four deep breaths saying 'relax' to yourself as you breathe out."

Practice   "Like any other skill, the more you practice, the better you'll become."

"You should practice both tensing and relaxing muscles and relaxing without tensing every day."

"Especially good times to practice are when you're waiting for something, before some event you want to be nice and loose for or when you're in bed at night."

"Practicing at night will help you get to sleep."

"You can practice during the day in such a way that no one will even know what you're doing."

Quick Tensing and Releasing

(Supplement)

Objective Students will engage in quick relaxation activity before beginning to work.

Strategy Tensing and releasing relaxation activity

Materials None

Procedure *Say or paraphrase the following:*

"Let's do a really quick relaxation exercise to get ourselves as relaxed as we can for our next activity."

"Close your eyes, take a deep breath, hold it, and tighten every muscle in your body."

"Scrunch up your whole body as tight as you can. Tell your neck and jaw to tighten."

"Tense your arms. Make fists with your hands, tighten up your stomach, your legs and feet."

"Hold every muscle as tight as you can. Hold it. Good!"

"Now breathe out and let go. Relax every muscle."

"Let the tightness just flow our of your body. Take a deep breath and say 'relax' as you breathe out."

"Now just quietly breathe in and out for a few moments."

"When you're ready, slowly open your eyes and we'll quietly begin our work."

Releasing Muscles to Relax

Objective   Students will learn to relax by releasing muscle groups.

Strategy   Students will use imagery and self-talk to relax muscle groups that tend to tighten under stress.

Materials   None

To the Teacher   See Activity #1

Procedure   *Explain to students the value of relaxation as outlined in Activity #1, then say or paraphrase the following:*

Relaxation sequence   "In learning to relax, the first thing I want you to do is to put your hands in your lap."

"I'd like you to choose either your right or left hand and I'd like you to look only at that hand and nothing else for right now."

"Now be sure your legs aren't crossed. Put your feet on the floor."

Right arm   "The first place we're going to try to relax is your arms."

"If your arms are relaxed, usually your whole upper body will be relaxed."

"I want you to talk directly to your arm muscles. First, talk to the upper part of your right arm."

"Tell it to relax, to just go limp. You might think it's relaxed, but let it go more—and more."

"Now relax the lower part of your right arm. Let it go until it becomes like a heavy weight on your leg."

Right hand   "Remember to be looking at your hand and nothing else. Now relax your whole right hand."

"Let it go utterly limp, just like a rag. Let your whole hand and arm feel like a heavy weight on your leg."

Left arm   "Now let's go over to your left arm. Talk to the upper part of your left arm."

"Tell it to relax, to just go limp. Now your left arm will begin to go heavy."

"Now talk to the lower part of your left arm and tell it the same thing."

"Just tell it to let go. Let it be loose and heavy."

Left hand   "Now talk to your left hand. Tell your hand to get that nice relaxed feeling."

"Check to see if both hands are relaxed and heavy."

"If your hands tingle a little bit, that's a good sign. A relaxed arm lets the blood flow right down into your hands and sometimes it tingles a little."

Eyes   "Now that you have your arms and hands relaxed, let's relax another part of your body."

"Let's work on your eyes. That may sound a bit strange, but there are six muscles around your eyes and relaxing them helps relax you all over."

"The first thing to do is to tell your eyelids to close."

"Don't try to close them. Just tell them to go gently down like two heavy black velvet curtains."

"Good! Now thank them for doing what you told them, and notice that they're beginning to feel pleasantly heavy again, and it feels good to let them be closed."

"Now let's work on relaxing your eyes. Just tell those six muscles that circle your eyes to let go."

"Feel your eyes just go loose and limp."

"Now that your eyes are closed and relaxed, I would like you to breathe very deeply and slowly."

"Take a deep breath . . . deeper. Let it out."

"As you breathe out, let yourself be more and more relaxed."

"Take a few more deep breaths and let them out. One . . . deep breath . . . two . . . let it out."

"One . . . deep breath . . . two . . . let it out."

Jaw

"Now let's relax the rest of your face muscles. Tell your jaw to relax."

"Just let it fall down a bit. Feel it getting loose and relaxed."

"If your jaw is relaxed, it's a good bet your whole upper body is relaxed."

"There is a slogan that's been given to many of the great athletes: 'No matter how fast you run, or how hard you try, keep your jaw loose and your hands loose.' "

"That slogan, 'Loose jaw—loose hands,' has helped break world records."

"So just let your jaw sag. Keep breathing slowly and deeply."

"Notice how you're getting more relaxed and slowly beginning to feel really good all over."

Shoulders

"Now tell your shoulders to drop as low as they will go. Don't pull them down."

"Just let them fall down. One of the headquarters of tension in your whole body is located in the back of your neck."

"This tension steals a lot of your strength and energy. You can wipe out the tension in the back of your neck by lowering your shoulders and dropping your head forward so your chin is nearly on your chest."

"Drop those shoulders even more. That's it. Get them way down."

"Did you feel the muscles in the back of your neck go limp?

"When you think you are really relaxed, let them go even more."

Chest

"Now let's relax your chest. Take a deep breath."

"Hold it. Whoosh . . . let it out."

"Just let your chest collapse. Let it sag."

"Imagine you are a big, heavy blob on the chair, like a big jellyfish."

"Breathe slowly. Each time you breathe, relax even more."

Stomach

"Let's relax the muscles of your stomach the same way."

"Tell your stomach muscles to let go. Don't try hard to do this."

"Remember, relaxation is like doing nothing. It's just letting the muscles go limp."

"That's good. You're all doing fine!"

Entire upper body

"At this point, most of you have reached a pretty good state of relaxation in the upper part of your body."

"Let's do a little detective work and see if we can find any hidden tensions."

"Take a quick search around for any tight muscles in your upper body."

"Every muscle should be limp and loose. Let everything sag comfortably."

"When you are completely relaxed, relax even more. Remember, do not try too hard."

"Don't force it. Just let go like a limp rag doll."

"We still have our legs and feet to relax."

Right leg and foot

"Talk to your right upper leg. Tell it to let go."

"Imagine there are no bones in your right leg. Make it become a heavy weight on the floor."

"Breathe deeply and slowly. As you breathe out, let go of any tightness."

"Now, let's go after your right lower leg. Just let it go."

"Your right foot should start to feel heavy on the floor."

"Breathe deeply and slowly. As you breathe out, let go of any tightness."

"Now, let's go after your right lower leg. Just let it go."

"Your right foot should start to feel heavy on the floor."

"Breathe slowly and peacefully. Relax all the muscles around your right leg and foot."

Left leg and foot

"Shift your attention to the upper part of your left leg."

"Get rid of any tensions there. Go completely limp."

"More . . . even more. Now your left lower leg; let it hang loose."

"Next relax your left foot. By now, both feet should be like heavy weights on the floor."

"Shift your attention to the upper part of your left leg. Get rid of any tensions there."

"Go completely limp. More . . . even more."

"Now your left lower leg; let it hang loose."

"Next relax your left foot. By now, both feet should be like heavy weights on the floor."

"You can probably notice a really good, warm feeling all over."

"When you're relaxed like this you'll find you can do things much better."

Conclusion

"By relaxing you can learn faster and remember things much longer. You can concentrate better."

"You can stay cool and confident no matter what—even if you have to do something really hard."

"Anytime you want to get relaxed in a hurry, say the word 'relax' and remember how you feel now."

"If you do this often enough, it can become a habit, and you can become automatically relaxed."

"Now I'd like you to slowly open your eyes, take a little stretch, and still hang on to that calm, relaxed feeling."

"For a first try, you did quite well."

"Some of you got into a fine state of relaxation really fast."

"Most of you made good progress toward being relaxed. A few of you, though, remained a little tense or tight."

"You hung onto your tight muscles as if they were old friends."

"Some of you kept opening your eyes. You were a little suspicious."

"I just want you to realize that learning to relax can't possibly hurt you in any way."

"It can do nothing but good for you. It can help you with school work, in sports, or with anything that worries you."

"Go along with us next time. Just give it a try."

Practice   "Like any other skills, the more you practice, the better you'll become."

"You should practice letting different muscles go limp several times a day."

"Especially good times to practice are when you're waiting for something or before a school, sports, or social event that you want to be loose and relaxed for."

"You can practice techniques in such a way that no one will even know what you are doing."

"Another good time to practice is when you are in bed at night."

"Practicing at night can help you get to sleep."

Muscle Releasing Relaxation Sequence

(Abbreviated Version)

Begin   "Let's do our relaxation exercises today, and let's make this the best re-laxation session we've had."

"I'm going to let you be more on your own today and relax some parts of your body by yourself."

"Here we go. Sit back in your chair and put your feet flat on the floor."

"By now you should be ready to close your eyes when we start our relax-ation session."

Arms   "Good. Now that all of you have your eyes closed, let's begin to relax our arms."

"Talk to your whole right arm first. Tell it to relax, to just go limp."

"You might think it's relaxed, but let it go more."

"Now let your hands be utterly limp, limp as a rag."

"Now your whole arm and hand should feel limp and heavy."

"Talk in the same way to your left arm and hand and get them totally relaxed."

"Remember relaxation is kind of like doing nothing. It's just letting go."

"I'll give you a few minutes to do this."

Eyes and jaw   "Let's relax your face muscles next. Let your eyelids feel like two heavy black curtains and let those six muscles that circle your eyes go loose and limp."

"Let your jaw feel loose and heavy. Let your whole face feel completely relaxed."

"I'd like you now to take some very deep breaths. Take a deep breath . . . deeper. Let it out."

"Another deep breath . . . deeper. Let it out."

"As you breathe out, let yourself relax. Do this two more times and this time tell yourself what to do."

Neck and shoulders
"Now tell your shoulders to drop as low as they can. Drop your head forward so your chin is nearly on your chest."

"Let the muscles in the back of your neck go limp."

"Now just imagine that you are a limp, heavy blob sitting on your chair."

"Let the whole middle part of your body just sag-g-g-g."

Legs and feet
"All we have left to relax are your legs and feet. Talk to the muscles of your whole right leg."

"Tell them to let go and completely relax. Your leg should feel limp and heavy."

"Your right foot should feel like a heavy weight on the floor."

"Remember to breathe slowly and peacefully. As you breathe out, let go of any tightness."

"Shift your attention to your left leg, and relax it by yourself."

"Tell your muscles to go limp and relaxed. I'll wait a bit while you do this."

"Good. Now you have two limp, heavy legs that are totally relaxed."

"You can probably notice a really good, warm feeling all over."

"Any time you want to get relaxed like this in a hurry, say the word 're-lax,' and remember how it feels to be really relaxed."

"If you do this often enough, you can relax yourself very quickly."

Practice
"Like any other skills, the more you practice, the better you'll become."

"You should practice letting different muscles go limp several times a day."

"Especially good times to practice are when you're waiting for something or before a school, sports, or social event that you want to be loose and relaxed for."

"You can practice techniques in such a way that no one will even know what you are doing."

"Another good time to practice is when you are in bed at night."

"Practicing at night can help you get to sleep."

Emptying the Sandbag

(Supplement)

Objective   Students will be able to quickly achieve a relaxed state in preparation for learning.

Strategy   Muscle releasing relaxation exercise

Materials   Sand in cloth bag (optional)

Procedure   You may wish to try this quick muscle releasing activity at times when students need to settle down in a hurry. If possible, show students what happens when sand begins to slowly seep out of a cloth bag. Emphasize just how limp the bag becomes. Say or paraphrase:

"With your eyes closed, focus on your right leg. Think of your right leg as if it were a sandbag."

"The sandbag has a hole in it, and all the sand is draining out."

"Feel the tension draining out of your right leg. Let the muscles go more and more."

"Let all of the sand drain from your right leg."

"Now think about your seat and your lower back. Begin to let these muscles go."

"The tension seems to pour out of those muscles like sand pouring from a bag."

"Think about your stomach. Begin to let those muscles go."

"Think about the tension draining out of your stomach the way sand might drain from a bag."

"Now think about your chest and back. Focus on those muscles and let them go."

"Focus on your shoulders and your neck. Begin to let those muscles go."

"Think about the sand draining from your neck and your shoulders."

"Feel how good it is to let go."

"Now your arms. Begin to let go."

"Think about the tension draining from your arms. Think about how you feel now that your body is relaxed."

"When you are ready, slowly open your eyes and begin to enjoy the rest of the day."

Becoming a Wet Noodle

(Supplement)

Objective   Students will be able to quickly loosen the muscles in their arms.

Strategy   Muscle releasing relaxation exercise

Materials   Wet noodles (optional)

Procedure   This activity is particularly good in helping younger students understand how to relax muscle groups. If possible, you might show students wet noodles to emphasize how limp you want students' arms to be.

Say or paraphrase the following:

"To play the 'Wet Noodle' game, you have to lay your head on your desk with one arm extended across your desk."

"Keep your extended arm limp as a wet noodle."

"I will now go around the room and check your arms to see how limp you can make them."

Go to one student and lift his arm. If it is related, praise him. Say:

"You are very relaxed, _____. Your arm feels just like a wet noodle."

Or:

"Your arm is not quite as loose as a noodle. Relax those muscles!"
"There, that's much better."

Go around the room and praise the students with the relaxed arms frequently. While you play the game, talk about some of the benefits of relaxation.

Source: Adapted from *The Solution Book: A Guide to Classroom Discipline*, by Randall Sprick.

Using Breathing to Relax

Objective   Students will focus on their breathing as a means of relaxing.

Strategy   Students use their own breath as the focus of their attention and count their breaths in sequences of 10.

To the
Teacher   A good way to quiet the mind or slow down circuit activity is to focus on breathing. Focusing on any one thing at a time is relaxing. The smooth ebb and flow of breath is a natural thing to focus on and the rhythm is itself calming. Since our breath is always with us, we always have a tool for relaxation close at hand.

Procedure   "Today we are going to use a very simple relaxation technique."

"It's very easy to learn. If you can count to 10, you can do it."

"First, make yourself comfortable. Sit in a chair with your feet on the floor."

"Keep your back straight. Try not to move during the exercise."

"Place your hands in your lap. Take a slow, deep breath. As you breathe in, count 'one' to yourself. All the way in."

"Then, slowly exhale, all the way out, and count '_____' to yourself. Silently."

"Another inhale is 'three,' out is 'four.' Quiet, deep breaths."

"In, 'five.' Out, 'six.' In, 'seven.' Out, 'eight.' In is 'nine,' out is 'ten.' "

"Keep counting. When you get to 'ten,' start over at 'one.' Slow, deep breaths. If you lose count, start over at 'one.' "

"Just count your breaths. If a thought comes, let it pass on by as if it were a gentle breeze."

"Just go on counting your breaths. Let any thoughts that float through your head go on out."

"Don't pay any attention to them. Don't let sounds bother you."

"Simply go on counting your breaths."

"When you get to 'ten,' start over at 'one.' If you lose count, start over at 'one.' "

Wait for several seconds, then continue.

"Just count your breaths. There is nothing else you have to do."

"If your attention wanders, just calmly bring it back to your breathing."

"Just relax, as you are. Keep counting your breaths."

"There is nothing you have to do. Just be here now."

"Let thoughts go by. Return to counting your breaths."

"When you get to 'ten,' start over at 'one.' If you lose count, start back at 'one.' "

"Now, when you're ready, you can stop counting your breaths and look up, and we will begin our work."

Short Breathing Exercises

(Supplement)

Objective   Students will engage in a short relaxation breathing activity so that they might calmly and quietly begin a learning task.

Strategy   Breathing relaxation exercise

Materials   None

Procedure   Choose one of the following breathing exercises as a quick way to calm students after an event that has left them keyed up.

1. Instant Relaxation

This exercise can be learned after achieving a degree of successful practice with progressive relaxation and counting breaths. Say or paraphrase the following:

"Draw in a deep breath and count to five slowly."

"Exhale slowly and tell all your muscles to relax."

"Repeat this step two or three times until you are more completely relaxed."

"Practice this instant relaxation skill anytime during your day when you want to feel relaxed instead of impatient."

"For example, while waiting in line."

2. Helium Balloon Breathing

"Sit comfortably in your chair and close your eyes."

"Imagine the area from the bottom of your stomach to your ribs is a bright colorful balloon that expands every time you fill it with air."

"First, exhale or breathe out deeply to let all air out."

"Then, inhale slowly and count of four, imagining the balloon filling with air from the bottom to the top as you do."

"Hold the breath for a moment (count of two). Exhale very slowly to the count of four, seeing the balloon slowly and completely deflate."

"Repeat this three or four more times."

3. Take a Deep Breath

"Lie down on the floor with your eyes closed."

If floor is carpeted, or if students can lie on jackets, do this:

"Feel the floor holding up your body. Take a deep breath all the way down to your stomach."

"Slowly let it out. Take another deep breath, and this time fill up your whole body and legs with air."

"Slowly empty out all the air. Lie quietly for a few minutes, breathing slowly and deeply."

"Open your eyes, and sit up slowly, and we'll begin our work."

Shaking Out Tension to Relax

Objective   Students will shake loosely and thus release muscle groups so that they are able to be attentive to classroom instruction.

Strategy   Students image themselves as rag dolls and shake their arms and legs loosely.

Materials   None

To the Teacher   Gently shaking large muscle groups tends to discharge tension and aids in relaxation and performance. Athletes often shake to loosen their muscles before an event. Runners in the Olympic games can be seen doing this before they run. Doing this exercise can provide students with a break from daily class routine. It enables them to return to work feeling more refreshed.

Because of the use of the image of a "limp rag doll," you may prefer to use this activity only with primary age children.

Procedure   *Have students remain seated while you say or paraphrase the following:*

"Sometimes when we are tired or tense, it feels good to let our muscles collapse and go loose and limp just like a rag doll."

"How does a rag doll's arm feel when we pick it up?"

Demonstrate with your own arm. You may wish to have a student show the class your arm is loose by lifting it and dropping it. Be sure it is loose!

"Make your arms floppy like a rag doll. If I pick up your arm, it should fall back down like this."

Try lifting a few students' arms that look relaxed.

"Doesn't that feel good? Now make your legs go floppy."

Demonstrate.

"If you pick up your leg, it should fall back down to the ground. Your arms and legs should be loose and floppy."

"Now let your head and neck go loose, as if you were a limp rag doll."

Demonstrate by rolling your head slowly and loosely in a circle from side to side.

Now demonstrate the following to students before having them do it: Bend at the waist and let your back gently bob up and down as your arms flop and swing. Let them flop and swing first directly in front of you, then to your left and then to your right. While you do this, say the following slowly in a "chant-like" manner:

> I'm a limp rag doll
> With no bones at all.
> My arms are limp.
> My legs are limp.
> I'm a limp rag doll.

When you mention your legs, let them bounce loosely. Invite students to do the exercise with you. Say:

"Doesn't that feel good? When you get tense or tired, if you just let your muscles go all loose and floppy like a rag doll, you can loosen up and then you'll feel more like continuing to work."

Using Visualization to Relax

Objective   Students will use visualization to achieve a state of relaxation.

Strategy   Students will relax their muscles while imaging themselves floating on a cloud.

Materials   White chalk, construction paper (optional)

To the Teacher   There are many ways to relax the body. It is not necessary to directly tense and relax muscles or focus on individual muscle groups and try to relax them. Students can use their thought processes to create visualizations that will result indirectly in a relaxed body. By using the "inner movies of their mind," students can become relaxed, calm and quiet. The use of visualization serves to attract attention and maintain interest. It doesn't matter a great deal what kind of visualizations are used. One of the reasons visualization can be relaxing is because, during a guided visualization, students direct their attention to picturing what the teacher says and cease looking at and thinking about other things. This slows down circuit activity. When circuit activity slows down, muscle groups become more relaxed. Thus, any direction of attention to one thing at a time is relaxing. Visualizing things that are intrinsically soothing while simultaneously telling muscle groups to go limp is even more relaxing yet.

The following is a relaxation exercise in which students visualize themselves relaxing on a cloud. You may want to make sure students can visualize a cloud by having them look out the window, if it's a cloudy day, or you could show a film of clouds.

You might do an art lesson on clouds, having students use the side of white chalk to make clouds. After the visualization they can draw themselves on one of their clouds and draw in other things they may have visualized.

Procedure   *Say or paraphrase the following:*
"Today let's experiment with some other ways to relax."

"First of all, I'd like you to get really comfortable in your chair."

"Put both feet flat on the floor and put your hands in your lap, but not touching each other."

"Just rest them comfortably on your legs."

"One good way to relax is to imagine certain things or make a 'movie' in our heads."

"When we do this, it's really important to keep our eyes closed so we're not distracted and so we can see really clearly the movie we're going to make in our heads."

"So now I'd like you all to close your eyes. Don't squeeze them shut."

"Just let your eyelids fall down like really heavy curtains. Let your eyelids feel as if they were just too heavy to lift."

A few students may find closing their eyes uncomfortable and may manifest this by giggling or making irrelevant remarks. It may be necessary to remind them that it's important that they keep their eyes closed for this activity, and that they not disturb others.

Begin to visualize

"Now imagine that it's a warm, sunny day and you're outside watching the clouds go by."

"As they float by, pick out one that you especially like."

Pause.

"Now imagine that you are sitting back on that beautiful, fluffy cloud."

"Feel yourself sinking into its softness as you slowly float along."

Relax

"Notice that your body is getting light. Feel your arms becoming light and limp."

"Now notice your legs feeling light and limp. Your legs feel as if they sink into the cloud."

"Now notice how light and limp your whole body feels as you sink back into the cloud."

"Notice how good it feels to have the cloud totally support you."

"Let your head just relax. Notice how good it feels to just let your whole body relax and sink into the cloud."

Breathe

"Take a big, deep breath. Hold it, and let it out."

Make audible sounds you would make taking a deep breath.

"Notice how you feel more relaxed each time you take a deep breath and let it out."

"Feel yourself drift along easily, slowly and relaxed."

Gently explore

"Feeling completely safe and secure on your cloud, look around."

"What things do you see? What things do you hear?"

Allow time for students to create their own visualization.

"When you're ready to come back to the room, take a deep breath and slowly open your eyes."

Discuss with students what they saw or heard from their cloud. Ask them if they feel any different now than they did when they came into the room.

The Sunshine Game

(Supplement)

Objective Students will learn a visualization/relaxation exercise that is calming and relaxing.

Strategy Teacher-directed visualization/relaxation exercise

Materials None

Procedure Explain to students that in this activity they will learn another visualization exercise that will relax them as well as give them constructive energy. Ask students if they understand the difference between constructive and destructive energy. An example of destructive energy would be where students use their energy in destructive ways, such as punching or hitting another person or in negative attention-getting behaviors. An example of constructive energy might include using the energy to complete a project, organize or clean a room, etc. The Sunshine Game provides for a nice visualization/relaxation exercise that calms and at the same time provides students with a constructive energy flow. Many times after lunch, students come in both hyped and tired. This exercise could be used after lunch recess to calm the class before beginning the afternoon studies.

Say or paraphrase the following:

"Lie on your back with your eyes closed."

"Be aware of your breathing."

"Take some deep breaths down into your stomach."

"Let your body become very heavy."

"Imagine a tiny speck of light in your stomach."

"Slowly let it expand."

"Watch it get bigger and bigger."

"Very slowly let it fill your stomach."

"Your stomach is now filled with light, energy, and warmth."

"Allow the relaxing light to spread throughout your body."

"It is like 'sunshine.' "

"You are filled with energy."

"You are calm and relaxed."

"When you are ready, open your eyes."

"Sit up rested and ready to begin to work."

Ask students to share what they felt from this exercise. How many could really feel the warmth of the sun in their stomachs? Did that feeling help to relax them? How many noticed a difference in their energy level as a result of this exercise? Can they really tell the difference between this self-induced energy as opposed to the energy they get from a candy bar or staying up too late at night and working on "nervous energy"? Explain to students that this is a nice exercise to do when they are uptight and tired, for it both calms them and provides them with needed energy.

Relaxing in the Forest

(Supplement)

Objective   Students visualize a walk through the woods as a form of relaxation.

Strategy   Teacher directed visualization/relaxation exercise; optional art and writing activity

Materials   Construction paper, colored markers (optional)

Procedure   Initiate this activity by asking students to list the sights, sounds, smells, and sensations of a forest. Ask students what they like most about the forest. Can sitting in a forest be a relaxing experience? When might it not be? Explain to students that they will visit the forest by using their mind. Their task is to create clear images centered on the theme "The Forest." Tell students that it is hoped their images of the forest will help to relax them.

Say or paraphrase the following:

Begin   "On your inner movie screen, create a picture of a portion of a forest."

Explore with your mind   "Allow your screen to expand as if you were watching a scene on television where the camera zooms back suddenly."

"Begin to notice all the varieties and thicknesses of the trees all around you. What is the color of their leaves?"

"The texture of their bark?"

"Notice the patches of sunlight that appear through the branches of the trees."

"What type of patterns do they make?"

"Feel the stones, the moss, the cool moist earth beneath your feet."

"Look up over your head to the soft green leafy cover."

"Notice the sky beyond."

"Observe the sounds and scents of life all around you."

"Reach out and touch the rough bark of a nearby tree."

Relax

"Lay your body down on a bed of moss."

"Look up at the tops of the trees. Notice how their branches try to catch a cloud."

"Allow your body to become very relaxed."

"Just let go and enjoy the smells, sights, sounds, and sensations of the forest."

After students have returned from their forest, ask students to share what they saw, heard, smelled, and felt. What images helped them to relax?

As an optional activity, ask students to draw the image they saw in the woods that most helped them to relax. Perhaps it was an image or a bird flying overhead. Perhaps the image that most relaxed them was seeing the patterns of sunlight through the branches. Encourage students to hang their drawings somewhere in their rooms where they can see them easily. It can be a reminder to relax.

Another optional activity is to have students write about their most relaxing image. Encourage students to vividly describe the image so that the reader can see the image, smell the smells, and hear the sounds. Share the writings with the rest of the class. Allow for class discussion to critique the writing. How effective were the writings in conveying the images the students saw in their minds? Encourage students to use this visualization whenever they are in need of relaxing or calming their mind.

Relaxing at the Beach

(Supplement)

Objective   Student will use visualization to reach a calm state of mind.

Strategy   Teacher-guided visualization/relaxation exercise, optional writing or art activity

Materials   Construction paper, colored markers (optional)

Procedure   Initiate this activity by asking students to list the sights, sounds, sensations, and smells of the beach. Ask students what they like about the beach. Explain to students that most people enjoy the beach because it is relaxing. Explain to students that you are going to take them to the beach by using the "inner movies" of their minds. Their task is to create clear images centered on the theme "Beach," and these are images that will also help them to relax.

Say or paraphrase the following:

Begin   "With your eyes closed, observe your inner movie screen."

"Allow the movie screen to go blank, as if you just turned your television off."

"Now on your screen you see your feet."

"You are standing on the sand."

Explore with   "Notice its color and texture."
your mind

"Follow the contour of the sand and the land down to the water's edge for as far as your inner eye can see."

"Do you see any trees, driftwood, dunes or dune grass?"

"Follow the beach to where it disappears around a bend into the ocean or on the horizon."

"Look in front of you."

"Can you see the ocean?"

"Is the water turbulent or smooth with small rippling waves?"

"Observe how the color of the water changes as you look outward to the horizon line."

Relax   "Allow the water to relax you."

"Allow that relaxing feeling to spread throughout your body."

"Look up at the sky."

"What color is the sky?"

"Allow yourself to float on top of a cloud, relaxing your entire body."

"See where the sun is and begin to feel its warmth."

"Let the heat from the sun penetrate your body until all your tension has melted away."

"Find your puddle of tension; watch the heat of the sun evaporate your tensions."

"Fill in all the details."

"The birds, other living beings."

"And then, create a blanket at your feet."

"Lie down on it, take a few deep breaths."

"Relax and enjoy your beach for as long as you like."

After students have returned from "The Beach," ask students to share what they saw at their beach. Did they become relaxed? What image helped them to relax the most? The sun or water?

Additionally, you may want to have students draw a picture of what they saw at their beach. Also, students could write a short description of what they saw at their beach. Encourage students to use this visualization of the beach whenever they need to "un-focus" their thoughts and relax.

A Relaxation Exercise That Would Relax Anybody

Objective   Students will cooperate in creating a relaxation exercise.

Strategy   Cooperative creative writing activity

Materials   Picture of tense person

Procedure   Divide students into small groups of four or five. Have them imagine that, as a group, they have been asked to create a relaxation exercise to help some extremely tense person.

Paint a picture of these persons for your students somewhat like the following:

"This person is so tense that whenever he picks up a pencil to write, he snaps it."

"His jaws are so tight that someone has to pry his mouth open with a screwdriver so he can eat."

"He grips the steering wheel of his car so tightly that he has to have someone pry his fingers off the wheel when he leaves the car."

"He breathes in such a shallow manner that his skin is blue."

"He's so stiff, you could use him for an ironing board."

"Your task is to write a relaxation exercise that will really work to relax this poor guy."

"Think of the most relaxing scenes you can and write them down in such a way that this guy can't help but loosen up."

Have students decide on one person in each group who will read the final draft of the group's relaxation exercise to the class.

Relaxation Bibliography

David, M., McKay, M., & Eshelman, E.R. (1980). *The relaxation and stress reduction workbook*. Richmond, CA: New Harbinger Publications.

Hendricks, G. & Willis, R. *The centering book*.

Keoppen, A.S. (1974). *Relaxation training for children*. Elementary School Guidance and Counseling.

McCamy, J.C., Presley, M.D., & Presley, J. (1975). *Human life styling*. Harper Colophon Books.

Osrander, S. & Schroeder, L. (1979). *Superlearning*. New York: Dell Publishing.

Richardson, F. & Woolfolk, R. (1979). *Stress, sanity and survival*. New York: New American Library.

Sprick, R. (1981). *A guide to classroom discipline: The solution book*. Science Research Associates.

Winter, B. (1981). *Championship performance in whatever you do: Relax and win*. La Jolla, CA: A.S. Barnes & Co.

Section E

Magic Tricks

List of Magic Trick Activities

Introduction

A collection of magic tricks has been included in this manual because they can be powerful tools for building self-esteem.

Teaching students magic tricks provides them with a "special skill" that they can share with their friends, family, and acquaintances. Students who are normally shy can become great entertainers through the vehicle of a magic trick. By teaching some of these tricks to students who are not well-accepted by their classmates, then having them perform the tricks (and even teach their classmates how to do them) makes these students feel they have something special to offer the class.

Several tricks are included that are performed by two people. A good technique to use with these is to choose a student who seldom "shines" in the class to be your partner and then the two of you can amaze the class.

Learning a magic trick can also serve as a positive reinforcer for appropriate classroom behavior. Learn a few of the tricks well yourself before you teach them to students and give students time and a place to practice the new tricks. Practicing a trick at least ten times or more without error is usually necessary in order to learn a trick well. Practicing in front of a mirror is also helpful. The tricks included here have all been used successfully with elementary age students.

You may wish to structure even more opportunities for students to build self-confidence by having students put on a magic show for a younger class.

These tricks can also be used as reinforcers to keep students on task during lessons. You can demonstrate a trick before a lesson and tell students those who stay on task during the lesson will get to see how the trick is done at the end of the lesson. This is an especially helpful technique for elementary counselors who go into classrooms and conduct guidance lessons.

Mind Reading a Message

The Trick

Distribute pieces of paper, all the same size, and have each person write short, one-sentence messages on them. After the messages are written, they should be folded twice and collected in a hat or a box. Tell the audience that you will read their minds and tell what they have written on the slips of paper. Then proceed to do so.

How the Trick Works

Pick up the first message, hold it to your forehead while you concentrate and then tell your audience that it says "I am the smartest person in the world." Ask who wrote it. No one will be able to claim it because you made it up. Unfold the slip of paper and nod your head as though you guessed correctly. but announce to the audience that they must admit when you read their minds from now on.

Pick up the next message and pretend to concentrate. Tell the audience what was written on the first slip of paper, the one you already opened. Ask the person who wrote it to identify himself. Then open the folded paper in your hand as if to check the words. (Actually, each time you are finding out what to say when you open the next message you draw from the box). Continue in this way until all the messages are read.

Since you will otherwise come out one slip of paper short, you must secretly return one as you take out the last of the actual messages. This is why you do not call attention to the number of papers handed out to begin with. If someone still has a question, tell him someone might have made out two messages instead of just one.

Magic Squares

The Trick

Put on the board or on a piece of tag board nine pieces of paper. Making them different colors will add to the mystery of how the trick is done. Arrange the pieces like this:

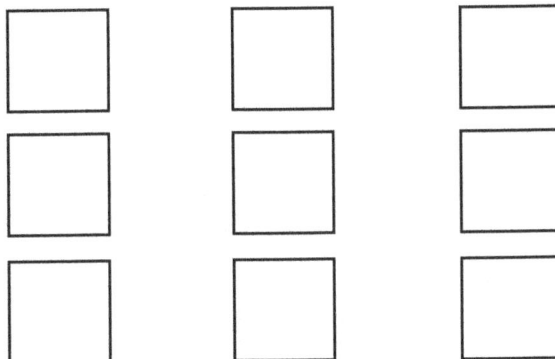

Choose one person to be your partner. Have the person leave the room. Ask someone from the audience to come up and simply point to one of the pieces of paper. Make sure everyone sees which piece was chosen. Call your partner into the room. Point to several pieces of paper, each time asking, "Is it this one?" Your partner will know when you point to the one selected while he/she was out of the room.

How the Trick Works

You will need to take a little time to train your partner before you do the trick. (You may want to train more than one person.) Explain to them that the nine little squares are arranged in a big square. Each little square is like a map of the big square. If someone chooses the square in the middle when your partner is out of the room, you will let your partner know this by pointing to the middle of one of the little squares.

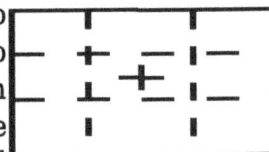

It doesn't matter which square you choose to give your partner the clue. The important thing is to point to the place on the little square that correlates with the position of the square chosen by the person from the audience.

If someone from the audience chooses a square in the top right hand corner, then you will indicate this to your partner by pointing to the top right hand corner of one of the little squares. If the square in the middle of the left side was chosen, show your partner this by pointing to the middle of the left side of any one of the little squares.

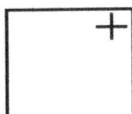

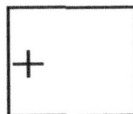

Explain that you will give the clue on the first square you point to. (You may not give the clue again.)

Tell your partner you will try and fool the audience by varying the times you ask "Is it this one?" You may ask this three times before you point to the right square. Another time you may ask this five times. Another time you may give your partner the clue the first time you point. For instance, if someone from the audience chooses the square in the lower right hand corner, you may point to the lower right hand corner of that very square and say, "Is it this one?" The answer your partner would have to give, of course, would be yes.

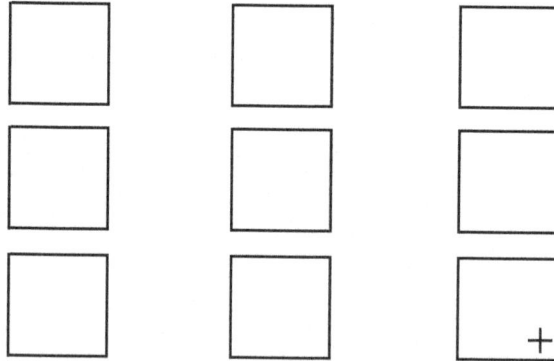

Tell your partner that the audience thinks you are using your voice to indicate which square it is. You may only point and say nothing. The trick will work just as well since the clue is in the pointing.

You may wish to ask the audience if they can try and guess how the trick is done. If they say they have a theory that holds up over three or four times, let them be your partner.

Message in Ashes

The Trick

Ask various people in the audience to call out their names and write each one down on a slip of paper. Fold each slip in half and drop it into a hat or a box. Five or six names are enough. Have a volunteer reach into the hat and take one of the names out. Put the remaining slips in an ashtray and burn them. Roll up your sleeve and rub some of the ashes briskly across your arm. A name will appear! Have your helper open the chosen slip of paper and read the name aloud. The name on your arm will be the same as the one read.

How the Trick Works

This trick takes a little preparation. Write the name of a member of your audience on your arm with soap. Cut a narrow piece of soap from the end of a bar, dip it in water, and write. When dry, the writing is invisible. This will turn out to be the correct name because when you write down the names, you write the same name on each slip of paper. Burning the papers destroys the evidence and makes ashes that will stick to the soap on your forearm.

The Magic Paper Clip

The Trick

Hold up a paper clip between your thumb and index finger. Wave your magic wand over it with your other hand and the paper clip disappears.

How the Trick Works

Attach a rubber band to the paper clip, while the other end of the rubber band is safety-pinned inside your shirt sleeve, up three or four inches. (Be sure to have a long-sleeved shirt on!) Hold the paper clip with the back of your hand toward the audience so they cannot see the rubber band. When you wave your wand over the paper clip. release it and the clip will instantly snap up your sleeve and disappear.

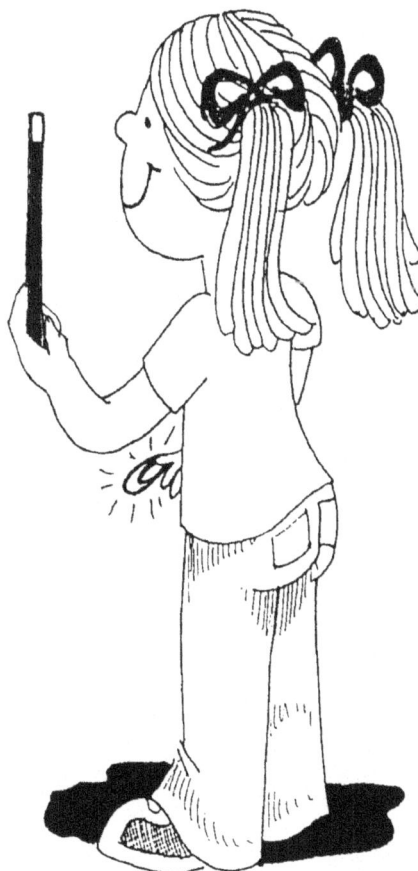

The Pharaoh's Finger

The Trick

Announce that you have something very special to show the audience. What you have, you say, came all the way from ancient Egypt. It was passed down from high priests and magicians until it finally came into your possession. Take a small box from your pocket as you tell the audience how, many years ago, robbers broke into the tomb of a great pharaoh and how the finger of the mummy pointed at them and left them cursed forever. The curse is still working and now <u>you</u> have the finger of that pharaoh. Open the box. There, resting on some cotton, is a real finger! Then, the finger moves. Quickly put the lid back on the box, looking frightened.

How the Trick Works

Cut a hole in the bottom of a small cardboard box and line the inside of the box with cotton. As you remove the box from your pocket, insert your own finger in the hole and bend it so that it rests on the cotton. The finger will look real so don't forget to wiggle it a little to scare the audience. If you look frightened at the end, those watching won't know what to think.

Source: *Magic Made Easy*, by Kettelkamp.

Magic Jumping Gum

The Trick

Show the audience that your hands are empty except for a single stick of chewing gum. Select a volunteer to help you with the trick, then put your hands behind your back for a moment. Explain that the gum is magic and will never be in the hand the volunteer chooses. Prove this by holding out both fists, palms up. Whichever hand the person chooses, the gum is in the other hand. Put your hands behind your back between each guess and let the helper pick several times.

How the Trick Works

You have an extra stick of gum hidden behind your back, in your belt or under the waistband of your pants or skirt. When you put your hands behind your back the first time, secretly put the extra stick of gum in your empty hand. Bring your clenched fists forward, hiding the gum in your palms, and ask your volunteer to guess which hand contains the gum. Whichever he or she chooses, you will show him or her the gum in the <u>other</u> hand and say, "Sorry, it's over here!" Put your hands behind your back each try and pretend to switch the gum from hand to hand. End the trick by hiding one piece of gum behind your back and giving the other stick to the volunteer for helping with the trick.

Boy or Girl?

The Trick

Tear a piece of paper into eight pieces and have two members of the audience write girls' names on four of the pieces and boys' names on the other four. Collect the slips of paper in a hat or a box. Have someone from the audience blindfold you. Reach into the hat, pick up a slip and tell the audience whether the paper has a boy's name or a girl's name written on it. Continue picking up pieces of paper until all have been identified as boys' or girls' names.

How the Trick Works

Tear the paper as shown in the illustration. The four pieces from the top and bottom will have two straight edges each, while the center four pieces will have only one smooth edge each. When you hand out the slips of paper, make sure the person writing the girls' names gets the four pieces with two straight edges, and the other four pieces will go to the second helper writing the boys' names. As you take a piece of paper from the hat you will be able to feel the edge of the slip to tell if the name is a boy's or girl's.

Mary	Sally
Tom	Mike
Barry	Frank
Lisa	Meg

Names in a Hat

The Trick

Ask five or six members of the audience to spell their names for you as you write them on individual note cards or pieces of paper. As you complete each card, fold it and drop it into a hat or a box. When all the folded papers have been deposited, ask someone from the audience to pick one out. Tell him to unfold it and look at the name without allowing you to see it. Concentrate for a moment, then tell the audience the name on the paper. Ask the assisting member to show the piece of paper to the audience to verify your answer.

How the Trick Works

Decide on just one of the six names spelled for you and write that one name on all the pieces of paper. The audience will think you are writing down each name as it is recited. When you tell them, "The name on the paper is . . . Frank!" no one will know that every folded paper has Frank's name on it.

Magic Chewing String

The Trick

Show your audience two pieces of string. Tell them you are going to chew the pieces into one single length of string. Put the two ends into your mouth and chew. You may wish to concentrate or look at your watch as if timing the process. When you have the full attention of the audience, take hold of one of the ends hanging from your mouth and slowly pull on it. One long piece of string will come from your mouth.

How the Trick Works

Use one long piece of string (about 14 inches) and one short piece (about four inches). Loop the short piece around the middle of the long piece, then conceal, between your thumb and forefinger, the place where the two lengths are looped. The ends of the short string will appear to be the ends of two long strings. When you pull on the end dangling from your mouth, you will be pulling the longer string through the loop. It will appear that you actually chewed two strings into one. (Conceal the short string in your mouth until you can get rid of it secretly.)

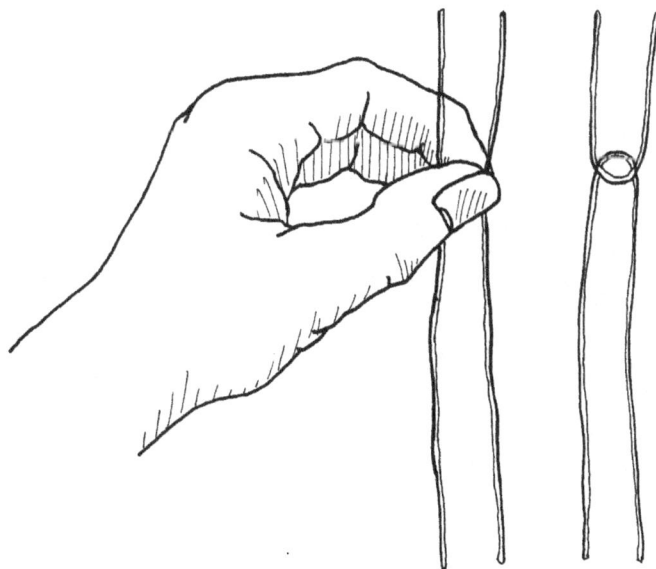

Penny and Teacups Trick

The Trick

Line up four teacups on a table so that they are clearly visible to the audience. Select a volunteer from the audience to be your helper. Then leave the room. The helper will then hide a penny under one of the teacups. When you come back into the room the teacups will be lined up as before. Concentrate for a few moments and then pick up one of the cups to reveal the penny underneath.

How the Trick Works

The volunteer you choose from the audience is really your secret helper. You will have already worked out a neat system for finding the penny. The teacups will have handles so your assistant can give you a clue. When you leave the room all the handles will be pointing the same direction. Your helper will hide the penny and then set the cup down with the handle in a different position from the others. To discover the penny all you have to do is see which teacup handle is different. You won't ever miss no matter how many times you do the trick.

The Linking Clips

The Trick

Fold a strip of paper so that its top edge has the shape of the letter "S." Put two paper clips on the top edge as shown in the diagram. Then pull the ends of the strip apart quickly. The clips will fly off and link themselves together. You can make chains of clips, too. Put the clip at the end of each chain on the slip of paper and have someone hold the other ends. When the slip is pulled apart the two chains will join into one.

How the Trick Works

Magician's Note: Believe it or not, there is no catch to the trick. As long as you put the paper clips on the slip of paper properly, the trick will work every time.

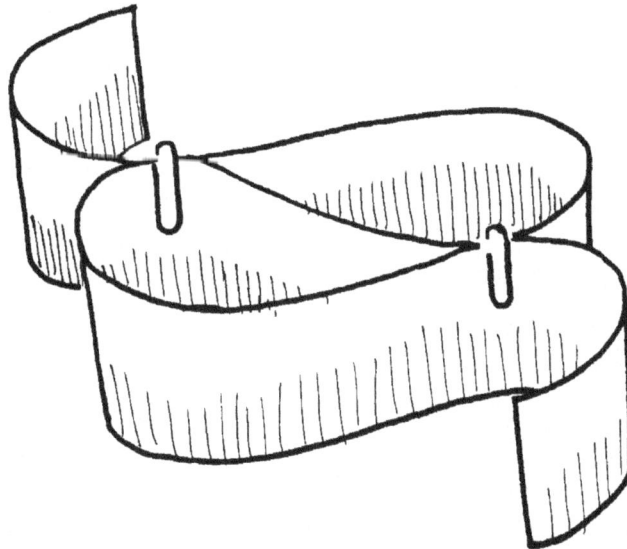

Bananamagic

The Trick

The magician brings out an ordinary banana. He or she asks the audience to select numbers from one to nine. The magician writes these numbers down on slips of paper and puts them in a box. A volunteer from the audience selects a number from the box. When the banana is unpeeled, it is found to be magically sliced into exactly that number of pieces inside the skin!

How the Trick Works

Find a banana that has several brown spots on the skin. Using a needle, puncture the skin of the banana and rotate the needle inside to slice the banana. Puncturing and rotating from both sides guarantees the slicing. Do this near both ends so that the banana is sliced into three even pieces. Dab off any juice that may ooze out of the puncture holes, which are otherwise almost impossible to see.

Now all that remains is to have the right number selected. Do this as follows: When you are writing down the audience-supplied numbers from one to nine, instead of writing the number that they select on the slips of paper, always write 3. This way the selected number will, of course, always be 3. (Be sure to casually get rid of the other slips of paper after the trick so that no one can examine them!)

Guessing the Object

The Trick

This is a two-person trick. The "mind reader" leaves the room while his or her assistant asks the audience to select three (or more) objects in the room. When the mind-reader returns, the assistant points to various objects in the room. The mind reader picks out each of the selected objects correctly.

How the Trick Works

The mind-reader and the assistant decide on a series of colors, such as red, white, and blue. When the assistant is pointing out objects in the room, the first selected object will be the one that is pointed to immediately after pointing to the first red object. The next selection will be the object after the next white object is pointed out. The last selection will be the one following the next blue object. This sequence can be kept up indefinitely, alternating red, then white, then blue. It is almost impossible for the audience to guess how the trick is being done.

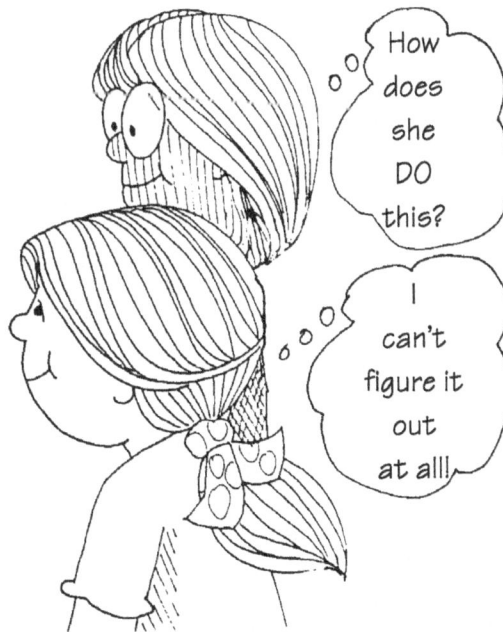

Finding the Hidden Paper Clip

The Trick

On a table are three identical opaque cups or glasses and a paper clip. While the magician is not looking, the paper clip is hidden under one cup and the other two cups are switched in position. When the magician turns around, he or she instantly is able to pick which cup the paper clip is hidden under.

How the Trick Works

The cups are not all exactly identical. Find some natural mark on one of the cups that makes it different from the others, or make a barely noticeable mark on it yourself.

Because the two cups without the paper clip have switched position, you can now determine where the clip is hidden. If your marked cup is in the same position as before you turned your back, then the other two cups have been switched and the clip is under your cup. If your cup has been moved, then it is empty and the other empty cup will now be in your cup's original position. Now the cup with the paper clip will be the one that is not marked and not where the marked cup used to be.

It doesn't matter which position the marked cup starts out in for the trick to work.

I Can Walk Through a Postcard!

How the Trick Works

1. Use a postcard.

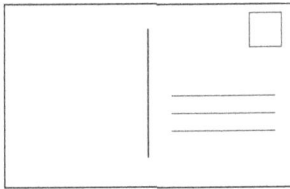

2. Fold it in half.

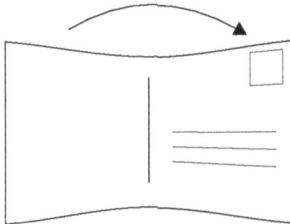

3. Cut along the dotted lines.
   (Not all the way to the end!)

   Do not cut these ends!

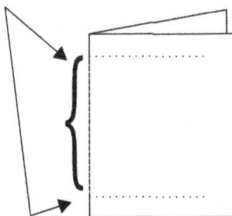

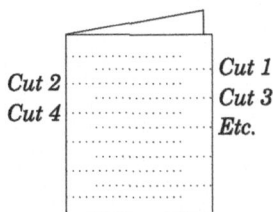

   Cut 2
   Cut 4

   Cut 1
   Cut 3
   Etc.

4. Carefully unfold the card and demonstrate that you can walk through the loop that you created.

> **NOTE:**
> **Make sure to practice at least once before you present this trick to the student audience!**

Magic Trick Bibliography

Kettelkamp, L. (1967). *Magic made easy* (4th Ed.). New York: Scholastic Book Services.

Norris, J.E. (1975). *It's magic*. Indianapolis, IN: The Saturday Evening Post Company.

Olney, R. & Olney, P. (1975). *Magic tricks*. Racine, WI: Western Publishing Company.

Tarr, B. (1977). *101 easy-to-learn classic magic tricks*. New York: Vintage Books.

Weatherby, J.C. (1962). *100 hours of fun*. Garden City, NY: Doubleday.

Windley, C. (1976). *Teaching & learning with magic*. Washington, D.C.: Acropolis Books.

Wyler, R. & Ames, G. (1968). *Magic secrets* (3rd Ed.). New York: Scholastic Book Services.

Bibliography

Bonoff, S. *Project Charlie*. Edina, MN.

Borba, M. & Borba, C. (1978). *Self-esteem: A classroom affair*. Oak Grove, MN: Winston Press.

Cautela, J.E. & Groden, J. (1978). *Relaxation*. Champaign, IL: Research Press.

David, M., McKay, J., & Eshelman, E.R. (1980). *The relaxation and stress reduction workbook*. Richmond, CA: New Harbiner Publications.

Dreikurs, R. *50 ways to maintain discipline in the classroom*. New York: Harper and Row.

Hendricks, G. & Willis, R. *The centering book*.

Hunter, E. (1972). *Childhood Education*. Report Cards for Teachers.

Keoppen, A.S. (1979). *Elementary school guidance and counseling*. Relaxation Training for Children.

Kettelkamp, L. (1967). *Magic made easy* (4th Ed.). New York: Scholastic Book Services.

McCamy, J.C., McCamy, M.D., & Presley, J. (1975). *Human life styling*. Harper Colophon Books.

Miller, N. (1975). *Testing & evaluation: New views*. Washington, D.C.: ACEI.

Nickerson, C., Lollis, C., & Porter, E. (1980). *Miraculous me*. Seattle, WA: Comprehensive Health Education Foundation.

Norris, J.E. (1975). *It's magic*. Indianapolis, IN: The Saturday Evening Post Company.

Ostrander, S. & Schroeder, L. (1979). *Superlearning*. New York: Dell Publishing.

Richardson, F. & Woolfolk, R. (1979). *Stress, sanity and survival*. New York: New American Library.

Smith, A., Cooper, J., & Leverte, M. *Giving kids a piece of the action*. Doylestown, PA: Tact.

Sprick, R. (1981). *The solution book*. Chicago: Science Research Associates.

Stevens, J.O. (1971). *Awareness: Exploring, experimenting, experiencing*, Moab, UT: Real People Press.

Tarr, B. (1977). *101 easy-to-learn classic magic tricks*. New York: Vintage Books.

Weatherby, J.C. (1962). *100 hours of fun*. Garden City, NY: Doubleday.

Wilt, J. & Watson, B. (1978). *Relationship builders*. Waco, TX: Educational Products.

Windley, C. (1976). *Teaching & learning with magic*. Washington, D.C.: Acropolis Books.

Winter, B. (1981). *Relax and win: Championship performance in whatever you do*. La Jolla, CA: A.S. Barnes & Co.

Wyler, R. & Ames, G. (1968). *Magic secrets* (3rd Ed.). New York: Scholastic Book Services.